AF413702

AWAKENING

to the

TRUTH

JERRY TROYER

Windan Sea Publishing
San Diego, California

ISBN: 979-8-9908307-0-7 (Hardcover)
ISBN: 979-8-9908307-1-4 (Trade Paperback)
ISBN: 979-8-9908307-2-1 (eBook)

Publisher's Cataloging-in-Publication
(Provided by Cassidy Cataloguing Services, Inc.)

Names: Troyer, Jerry (Jerry Stephen), author.
Title: Awakening to the truth / Jerry Troyer.
Description: San Diego, California : Windan Sea Publishing, [2024]
Identifiers: ISBN: 979-8-9908307-0-7 (hardcover) | 979-8-9908307-1-4 (trade paperback)| 979-8-9908307-2-1 (ebook)
Subjects: LCSH: God (Christianity) | God--Proof. | Deism. | Belief and doubt--Religious aspects-- Christianity. | Spirituality. | Faith. | Skepticism--Religious aspects--Christianity. | Self-actualization (Psychology)--Religious aspects--Christianity. | BISAC: RELIGION / Christian Living / Personal Growth. | RELIGION / Christian Living / Social Issues. | RELIGION / Faith Deconstruction.
Classification: LCC: BT103 .T76 2024 | DDC: 231--dc23

To Gene who taught me that I must live 2 Corinthians 1:3-7,

with all the compassion in my heart.

Contents

PROLOGUE

ALL PEOPLE HAVE BEEN created by God, yet many question God's existence. Disbelieving in God leads to people thinking they know better or are smarter than God. In fact, many believe they would run the world better than God. They tell themselves they would not let the innocent be harmed by others. They would ensure there were no more natural disasters, racial inequities, pandemics, or sin.

Almost all of us look for our place in this world. We started our lives with hopeful hearts that were full of dreams. Somewhere during life, we started wondering about achieving the fulfillment and pleasure we desire so deeply.

Sometimes we feel we are standing still and that the pages of our lives are never turned. In truth, above all our conflicting emotions, imperfect judgments, or broken dreams, there is a kingdom above all the wonders the world has ever known. There is a God that will give us all the riches and treasures of heaven if we believe in Him. When we believe in God, worship Him, pray to Him, and seek forgiveness from Him, we find there is no way to measure the worth of how God's Son died for us. When God's sacrifice was rejected,

He took the fall and thought of us.

When you think you could do a better job than God, remember that God was here before the world began. He provides us with all the wisdom and ways of man. He is above all nature and created all things. God's power is endless, above all kings and beyond every power on Earth.

Chapter One

THE REBEL HEARTS OF ADAM AND EVE

GOD CREATED ANGELS. THERE was an angel of greater beauty than all the others. One with a melodic, lovely voice. An angel assigned to serve God in mighty ways. However, this angel wanted more, more than any other angel imagined. This angel was proud, utterly selfish, and coveted God's power. Time passed, and with it, this angel decided he must have the power of God so he could reign both Heaven and the world. He grew to hate God. He began a campaign to turn all the angels away from God. Away from the God that created them. The angel's name was Lucifer, but we often call him the Devil here on Earth. Some of the angels listened and followed Lucifer. However, the majority of angels stayed faithful to God.

It was only a matter of time before Lucifer, also known as the Devil or Satan, was cast out from Heaven to Earth. God did not destroy Lucifer as He could have. Rather, God told Lucifer he was banished from Heaven and would have to roam the Earth until the war was over. This war is what we live in every day, and it manifests itself every time we sin. Every time there is a war, a fight, then hate can grow in our hearts. As we battle to live in the light of God's love we see there will be a cataclysmic war between God and Satan at God's appointed time. While we struggle to do good every day, Satan wants the exact opposite from us. Satan roams the Earth looking for people who will believe him and his lies. The Devil seeks to keep all people from following God or keep them from further advancing God's kingdom. There are billions of people, including some within our own families who have fallen prey to Satan without even knowing it. Satan's greatest desire is for us to spend eternity with him, experiencing great torment in hell. He never wants us to go to heaven to spend everlasting pleasures with God.

The first people God created after the world was formed were Adam and Eve. He gave them control and responsibility over everything. Yes, everything. He loved them so very much. He gave them more than they would ever need. He gave them a life with gifts beyond what could be imagined. And He gave them everything with His love.

God did set a rule to follow or a code of conduct for their day-to-day life. There was only ONE rule. There was one stipulation, just one. God told Adam and Eve to never eat from the tree of knowledge of good and evil. That was all. They could do everything else they wanted, dreamed of, or imagined. God had given Adam and Eve a paradise on Earth.

It was the most beautiful place on Earth, and it was named, "The Garden of Eden." Adam and Eve lived in the Garden of Eden, the paradise that God created. There they lived in complete joy and happiness. Adam and Eve had no problems, felt no sorrow, and never had to worry about illness and death. They lived in perfection without knowing it. God visited them daily, and they loved the visits. God was wellpleased, and collectively, God, Adam, and Eve loved one another and the life God created and gave them.

Then one day, Satan came to the garden. Satan had been watching them all from afar and saw how God loved Adam and Eve. Satan became enraged, watching God with Adam and Eve. All Satan wanted was to destroy that love. He wanted to destroy the life Adam and Eve lived in the perfect paradise God gave them, so he concocted an idea to deceive Eve.

One day he visited Eve in the Garden of Eden. Satan disguised himself so Eve would not recognize him and began to tempt Eve into disobeying God. Satan convinced Eve that God was not being a good God and was not treating them as He should. Satan went on to say that Eve and Adam deserved better because God was not being fair to them. Satan kept the most powerful temptation until the end. Satan told Eve that they should know everything that God knows. The only reason God did not want them to eat from the tree of knowledge was that

He did not want them to be as powerful as He was. He posed the thought, "Why shouldn't they know as much as God?"

So Eve began to forget all God had given them. She forgot that everything they had was because God created it for them, from the oceans that push and pull at God's command to the breath they drew from the air around them. God had the voice that calmed the sea and had given Adam and Eve His love and joy. He heard them every time they called Him. He caught them when they fell, and most of all, He told them who they were and why they always had His love. However, Eve forgot all of that as Satan tempted her to eat from the tree of knowledge.

Satan used the tree of knowledge as a weapon. Satan told Eve that if she ate of the tree of knowledge, she would know everything God knows and become equal to Him. Eve bought into the deception and reasoned that she wanted to be treated fairly and deserved equality with God. In a moment, she wanted to have what she thought she deserved. Amazingly, Satan deceived her in three sentences. Imagine what he does to us with the unlimited words, emotions, events, people, and sins he created to keep the whirlwind of chaos and deception swirling around us.

So Eve ate the fruit, and it was good. Her eyes were open to see things in a new way. She saw such splendor and learned so much that she gave the fruit to Adam, and he ate it as well. After all, Adam reasoned with Eve and wanted to be treated fairly too. Adam also wanted to be equal with God.

One of the first discoveries they made and understood was that they were naked. Never before did they know or care, so ever since that date, humankind has dealt with covering their nakedness.

God came to visit Adam and Eve that evening as usual. However, that evening Adam and Eve hid from Him. God asked where they were, although He already knew where they were and what they had done. Adam answered that they were hiding because they were naked. Then God confronted them about what they had done by eating from the tree of knowledge. Adam admitted it but projected the blame onto Eve. After all, it was Eve whom Satan had deceived. So Adam blamed Eve, and Eve blamed Satan, and in that one moment, the life God had planned for them and for all humanity was over. There would never again be life in the Garden of Eden paradise or a life without end. At least not until God's son Jesus returns to Earth again.

God cast Adam and Eve out of the Garden of Eden for their sins. Adam and Eve would also have to wear clothes made from animal skins. God told them they would now experience joy and pain. They would keep love but experience agony. Eve would have great pain bearing children. Adam would have great difficulty growing crops for food. The suffering for both of them would test their strength and hurt their heart. However, the very worst thing they would experience was death. They would no longer live for eternity but would die with no one ever knowing when death would come for them.

Chapter Two

INEVITABLE

ADAM AND EVE ALWAYS had the memories of all they had and all they lost. Memories become part of our lives, and memories can bring us down or pull us up. God allowed us to hold onto our memories in the hope that we would begin to learn the difference between what was good and what was sinful. It is intended that we make good choices based on love and God's word. It was God's wish for us to live in the light of his love. Instead, many of us choose to worship God with the least effort possible. We want God to read our minds but not our hearts. We do not want to hear the word of God unless it comes from a rock star preacher who tells us our blessings are in our pockets and wallets. That all we have to do to receive the blessings is give them money because only then will goodwill and fortune come to us.

Many people will not cross the street if someone is in pain because we tell ourselves it is not our problem. We also tell ourselves that since God lives in churches, the religious leaders of those churches need to set hearts free. In reality, every change has to start with us through our prayers for God's intervention. We need to change the inevitable darkness of a sinful life by walking a mile in someone else's shoes. We need to change the inevitable sorrow of the world by understanding that the church and God's words from Sunday still exist on Monday.

For us to get to a place where we can succeed in finding God and His message, we have to start by understanding what happened to Adam and Eve and their two boys after being cast out of the Garden of Eden by God.

The older son was named Cain, and he became envious of Abel, the younger son, because Abel loved and pleased God. In return, Abel received God's love. Cain did not receive the depth of God's love because he did not love God. So one day, in a fit of jealous rage, Cain killed his brother. So murder entered the world we live in today. We all know premeditated murder is a sin and that God hates sin. Yet we still have murders occurring every day of the year throughout the world.

Since those times, humanity has struggled against each other, warred with other nations, and fought those they labeled enemies. As centuries went on, almost all humankind stopped following God as their Lord. So, God sent prophets to the people. God sent prophets to the people and instructed them that humanity should turn back to Him. The prophets reminded the people that they should love God and return to ways of following and living for Him. God spoke through the prophets. He sent words of how much He loved us and wanted to give us if we would simply follow Him, accept Him, and love Him as our Lord. But God did not stop there. God also gave words to the prophets that told humanity what would happen if they did not follow Him, return to Him, love Him, worship Him, and live for Him.

Some people listened to the prophets and said they would surrender their pride and turn from sinful ways. Many people knew God would hear prayers in Heaven and forgive our sins. But the majority of humankind did not listen to or follow God. Yet God still did not give up on us. On the contrary, He remained patient and faithful to humanity. He gave us opportunities to live abundantly faithful lives honored Him.

He let us know if fear weighed on us, and we reached out to God, He will be for us. God has always available for us. When we lifted our eyes up to the Lord we witnessed God who takes down giants and mountains are moved. We know God makes water part, yet even that did not ensure that people would listen and obey God. Many people created gods they could create and worship. Non-living gods that they could use for their own purposes.

Then, God whispered a warning to us that most people did not heed. God told us there would come a day when He would take action against people because of their non-belief. God would take action because people who did not or would not listen or turn back to him, even when eyes witnessed God's power, still did not turn back to Him. That brought humankind and the world to a perplexing, painful, and seemingly unending set of problems.

Why would a God of love allow His people to hurt? Why would a God of love let them die painful or early deaths? Why does God allow bad things happen to good people? Especially the innocent like children? There is no exact answer because God is God and there is no other like Him. He does not answer to you, me, or any other human. He is God.

This we do know, God created a perfect world, without evil or disease or anything not perfect. He had a great desire to have a relationship with a being other than angels. A relationship with persons. What we call mankind today. He created Adam and said it was very good. He then created Eve to be his soulmate and helper.

God gave a great gift to Adam, Eve, and all people. As said earlier, He gave them the gift of free will. A gift He did not retract.

God was saddened at the beginning, with the development and ongoing depravity of the world through all the generations. But He did not change His unbreakable commitment to let people have free will.

Each one of the nearly eight billion people in the world has free will. Some use their free will for good. Many do not. A lot of people use their free will for only their benefit. There are people who look to do harm and vile things. That is the core reason why evil, bad, depraved, and disgusting things that happen in this world.

I do know He loves all. He wants all people and children to spend eternal life with Him in love and light. He is our Creator and giver of all life. It is apparent God hates evil and depravity. He does not allow it in His presence. Yet, He provides us a way to find forgiveness and redemption for the sinful things we do. Through it all He loves us with more love than we can fathom, but He will want us to turn from self-centered, me-only lives, and establish hearts of love for Him.

Chapter Three

GENIUS

L ET US LOOK as if you are god in this particular situation.

In this story, you are the Creator of all. You have created everyone.

People are formed through sex. You oversee it and allow creation of beings. You have provided different people with different gifts,so they can use them to serve you in special ways. If you had made everyone the same, would there be the joy, and would there be the uniqueness of individuality? Life would be mundane, boring, without much reason to live. Every day is a repeat of the previous. You made everyone unique, special, and gifted with special abilities. Some will be CEO's. Some have beautiful singing voices; some will be prolific parents. Some will be great gardeners. On and on. Some will be less talented. People will look at them with disdain and categorize them as lessor or a waste.

Some will struggle with emotional issues. People will address them as weak and unworthy. Others will just be normal, average people. They will not be easily respected by their peers, for the world wants to honor the special ones.

One year you create a special boy who is given the name Genius.

He has the ability to change the world.

As Genius grows, he is studious and dedicated to learning. His comprehension and recollection are amazing. Nobody has ever been like him. He spends his time being absorbed with learning. He quickly advances through school and finishes college at age 13. With his excellent skills, he develops into a first-rate scientist. He probes, studies, and deduces the events of the world and human creation. Through his research and some required assumptions, Genius comes to the conclusion that you did not create the world or create humans.

The world was created by a huge gargantuan big bang. A cosmic event that has never happened before or since. It will never be repeated.

As for humans, Genius defines a process whereby the human has evolved from the scales of a fish. He is so intelligent that people start listening to him. They recognize his brilliance and the easily influenced have no option but to believe. They don't seek an answer from you as to whether Genius is correct in his conclusions. Instead, they turn their beliefs toward him, and move away from what you have informed them in your book, "Counsel." The book that you provided to guide them. Your book "Counsel" is the guide for all people. It instructs on how to live lives to receive good benefits. Through their belief and worship and service to you.

Since Genius is a visible man, is human and right before their eyes, they see and believe him. While they have no means of proving whether such conclusions or processes could happen, they believe. They turn to follow the man and turn away from you.

People want the best, the very best life can offer. They believe that if they follow Genius, life will be better. Life wasn't so good when they were following you. They can hear Genius and he makes sense to them. People do not even seek unequivocal proof. He is beyond a genius and a scientist too. He has to be right. To heck with you. People can't see you. They can't hear you. There are people who speak about you and the writings in "Counsel." But they can't prove that what "Counsel" says is absolutely true. Besides, it is ancient. Times have changed. You, you haven't updated "Counsel"...ever! If it ever was true and accurate, it can't be anymore. You are out of time, out of tune, and simply not current. They say "Counsel" just doesn't apply to us.

People enjoy the newness, freshness, and theories of Genius. He becomes a leader by means of his great charisma. People fall in line behind him. Absorbing every thought he utters as truth and right. Soon, the vast majority of the world has turned to following Genius. They have left you behind.

You who created each and every one of them. You who created the world for their pleasure, so they would recognize Your love. The result should be that all would willingly and totally love you, by their free choice, and live for you.

Yet now they are following Genius, who is not with you. He is against you. And says so. He makes it very clear you are not God. Humans have evolved and then procreated. Evolution will continue, even though he has great difficulty showing how humans have evolved in the last 100 years. This man is adamant that you did not create the world people live in. The man gives his scientific evidence to prove it was not you who created the world.

Genius believes and expounds on how you do not exist. You are just made up. You aren't real. No god would require things that you require; worship, praise, adoration, living life to love you and others. Genius says that you just can't be real. He commands that if you were, you would be delighted to give everything to everyone as they want it.

In addition, Genius says, that you need to make everything clear. He demands that you cannot or will not prove that everything you have said or written is true. Genius believes he can and does. However, as scientists investigate Genius's work, they must make assumptions (unproven assumptions) to make his calculations and theories true.

Then one day Genius dies. Will the people put aside the man's work and theories because he could not keep from dying? He, as a scientist, could not find a means for him to continue living. Why? He should have been able to. He was a genius.

Since he is no longer existing, shouldn't the people be returning to you? Your book "Counsel" says you are continual, never ending. Which is true. However, the people would rather believe the dead man's theories and ideas rather than turn back to you.

You as God

Now what do you do? The people do not love you. Worship you. Or serve you. They have each turned away from you to believe what a man has said. A man you created and allowed to live. You gave him the opportunity to come to you every day of his life. Even up to his last day. But he did not.

What will you do? How do you bring these people back to you before their demise so they can spend eternal life with you? "The words" say there is eternal life. All people will either spend joyful eternal life with you or have eternal life in a dark, dreadful abyss with continual pain and anguish. Living only with others who never came to believe in you. As you have said in "the words," they will never have another opportunity to come to you after their life ends because they rejected you and said so. You cannot fathom why they would think that. You have proved you created them.

What do you do? Kill all those who don't believe in you? Start over? Stop free will by a simple wave of your hand? Create only humans who will honor you? Or do you allow people to live against you? Even those who proclaim you are not god. They say that you are not the Creator of humans and the universe.

You have to decide. It is your choice. Which will it be? Are you going to let them go on living with their thinking, which is against you? Will you still give them an opportunity to come to you even up to the day of their last breath, even though they defame you?

You have sent messages they cannot miss. Messages await them in the "Counsel". Also you sent messages through those who have spoken of their belief in you. Or do you need to be a great magician and show them an act they will not be able to avoid believing?

What will you do?

At last, you decide. You will wipe out all those who don't believe in You as their creator and god. Then you will let the remaining believers procreate a new generation of followers, who will grow up and worship you as god.

What the True God Will Do

God's word never changes. He has created all and formed everything. Earth, sky, oceans, cosmos, stars, and celestial objects (Genesis 1:1-2:25). He will continue to allow each person their own free will and choices up until the day they die.

God has decided to bless the non-believers, along with believers. He provides them sun and the splendor of all creation. He provides them love and opportunities. He also allows pain and suffering in the lives of believers and unbelievers.

Interestingly, when you look at the Bible you see the first people created, Adam and Eve, were completely content doing the things God had them doing in the garden of Eden. They weren't complaining to God or fighting each other or wishing for a more challenging, rewarding job. That is until "The Enemy" came into the picture.

God respects all people. If you elect not to believe in Him, He will allow it. It will break His heart, but He will allow it. If you reject Him, He will reject you (Romans 1:18-20,24-25, Acts 7:39-42a, Deuteronomy 8:19). Everyday of your life He will send signs, wonders, information, and opportunity for you to turn to Him, believe in Him and ask His Son, Jesus the Savior, to be your God (Matthew 5:44-45, Deuteronomy 8:18). He may use circumstances and consequences to get your attention and focus, but He has determined that He will not command your obedience to Him. Nor mandate belief in Him. It is your choice. If your decision is to not follow Him, He will grant you separation from Him for eternity. Then there will be no reconsideration. No second chance. He will oblige you by sending you to hell. The place you would rather be than to honor, serve, follow, obey, and love God the Father, Jesus the Son, and the Holy Spirit.

Once you reside in hell and you decide you hate hell, where there is weeping, crying, and gnashing of teeth, you will have no option of getting out. Even if you want to change and think there may be a chance for you to get out, there will not be such a chance. Even if you say you will give believing in God a chance, you will not be granted that option. You are in hell forever (Revelation 20:10-15)!

When you are conflicted and misery abounds in hell you will not have the availability to warn your living family, friends, and relatives to seek out God. They are receiving the same availability of receiving God every day that you had.

Neither you, yourself, nor anyone in hell will be able to bridge the chasm between heaven and hell. Nor will anyone in hell find a means to breech the boundaries of earth from the depths of hell once hell is closed forever. Here is what God says through His inerrant word. God addresses that in the Book of Luke 16:19-31.

Genesis 1:1 In the beginning God created the heavens and the earth. 2 The earth was formless and empty, and darkness covered the deep waters. And the Spirit of God was hovering over the surface of the waters.

Genesis 1:25 God made all sorts of wild animals, livestock, and small animals, each able to produce offspring of the same kind. And God saw that it was good.

Romans 1:18-20 But God shows his anger from heaven against all sinful, wicked people who suppress the truth by their wickedness. [i] 19 They know the truth about God because he has made it obvious to them. 20 For ever since the world was created, people have seen the earth and sky. Through everything God made, they can clearly see his invisible qualities—his eternal power and divine nature. So they have no excuse for not knowing God.

Romans 1:24-25 So God abandoned them to do whatever shameful things their hearts desired. As a result, they did vile and degrading things with each other's bodies. 25 They traded the truth about God for a lie. So they worshiped and served the things God created instead of the Creator himself, who is worthy of eternal praise! Amen.

Acts 7:39-42 But our ancestors refused to listen to Moses. They rejected him and wanted to return to Egypt. 40 They told Aaron, Make us some gods who can lead us, for we don't know what has become of this Moses, who brought us out of Egypt. 41 So they made an idol shaped like a calf, and they sacrificed to it and celebrated over this thing they had made. 42 Then God turned away from them and abandoned them to serve the stars of heaven as their gods!

Deuteronomy 8:19 But I assure you of this: If you ever forget the Lord your God and follow other gods, worshiping and bowing down to them, you will certainly be destroyed.

Revelation 20:10-15 Then the devil, who had deceived them, was thrown into the fiery lake of burning sulfur, joining the beast and the false prophet. There they will be tormented day and night forever and ever. 11 And I saw a great white throne and the one sitting on it. The earth and sky fled from his presence, but they found no place to hide. 12 I saw the dead, both great and small, standing before God's throne. And the books were opened, including the Book of Life. And the dead were judged according to what they had done, as recorded in the books. 13 The sea gave up its dead, and death and the grave[a] gave up their dead. And all were judged according to their deeds. 14 Then death and the grave were thrown into the lake of fire. This lake of fire is the second death. 15 And anyone whose name was not found recorded in the Book of Life was thrown into the lake of fire.

Luke 16:19-31 Jesus said, There was a certain rich man who was splendidly clothed in purple and fine linen and who lived each day in luxury. 20 At his gate lay a poor man named Lazarus who was covered with sores. 21 As Lazarus lay there longing for scraps from the rich man's table, the dogs would come and lick his open sores. 22 Finally, the poor man died and was carried by the angels to sit beside Abraham at the heavenly banquet. The rich man also died and was buried, 23 and he went to the place of the dead. There, in torment, he saw Abraham in the far distance with Lazarus at his side. 24 The rich man shouted, Father Abraham, have some pity! Send Lazarus over here to dip the tip of his finger in water and cool my tongue. I am in anguish in these flames. 25 But Abraham said to him, Son, remember that during your lifetime you had everything you wanted, and Lazarus had nothing. So now he is here being comforted, and you are in anguish. 26 And besides, there is a great chasm separating us. No one can cross over to you from here, and no one can cross over to us from there. 27 Then the rich man said, Please, Father Abraham, at least send him to my father's home. 28 For I have five brothers, and I want him to warn them so they don't end up in this place of torment. 29 But Abraham said, Moses and the prophets have warned them. Your brothers can read what they wrote. 30 The rich man replied, No, Father Abraham! But if someone is sent to them from the dead, then they will repent of their sins and turn to God. 31 But Abraham said, If they won't listen to Moses and the prophets, they won't be persuaded even if someone rises from the dead.

Chapter Four

SPECTACULAR

YOU HAVE GIVEN PEOPLE an opportunity to lead. You have set people in a place of power. Initially, they were grateful for such an honor. Now they are acting against you. They are mistreating others you have created. Those being mistreated are angry at you for putting this leader in place. They are so angry they are totally turning away from you. You provided a special gift of wisdom, understanding, and knowledge to the one called Spectacular. She had asked you for those gifts and you had blessed her with them. Not only those gifts but, because she did not ask for beauty, or wealth, or long life, you gave her all those things in immense abundance. You expanded her territory and the people under her loved it. She ran for the highest office in the land and you availed upon her with a great victory. Spectacular became the most influential person in the world. She was serving you well. She meditated upon you. She sought you in prayer and sacrificed to you, looking in all ways to honor you with her life. People were amazed at the wisdom she beheld. Other government leaders yearned to have an audience with her. Seeking her counsel on any and every subject. She amazed the leaders with her expert opinions and beliefs. All her responses hit the center of the mark. She was revered globally. The people that elected her adored and worshiped her. Never before had their lives been so good. Taxes were low and loss of lives in wars were minimal. The economy flourished under her tutelage. Never before had an approval rating been so high. She had very few opponents, political opponents. The previous election was the greatest landslide in the history of all records. In her latest reelection she had no opponent. She was infamous.

Over time she began to listen to those who were near her. Those people who did not follow you or accept you as their eternal Savior. They thought it was quite ludicrous to be obsessed with you and worship you. They believed they had brains for a reason. It was not to appreciate or bow down to you. They had the strength, the wit, the might to carry on by themselves and make monumentally appropriate decisions. They did not need you.

Slowly, yet with increasing success, they were turning the mind of Spectacular toward their way of belief. Belief in self. She began to seek out things for her pleasure. She had desires and she decided it was time for her to experience and enjoy some of them. No, not some of them, all of them. She had sacrificed so much for so long. She kept asking, contemplating thoughts about herself and wondering that certainly it must be time she got to enjoy some of the finer things in life. That it had to be her turn to enjoy some of the good things of life. She convinces herself that it would certainly be fair.

Down the road of self-indulgence she went. Paying less attention to the situations and needs of her kingdom. Leaving many decisions to her underlings. Spending more time focusing on pleasures in her life. She was not in the office much or attending to governmental business. She was riding high on her popularity and newfound pleasures.

Over time the people of the country began to wonder about her. Was she alright? Has something happened to her? What had happened to the bright, charming, effervescent, wise leader? She seemed so different. Talked differently than before. Spoke down to people. Acted superior. Her popularity and approval rating started to languish. Journalists began producing work that included innuendos of Spectacular's change in government operation. Spectacular saw those articles and was incensed. Yet she had little time for trivial things. She was having a delightful time living the good life. She could do anything she wanted, anytime she wanted, in any way she wanted. Her morals lowered and she left her husband and children behind. She found other men who worshiped her.

In the coming days, she wanted all the people to continue loving her and be addicted to her greatness. However, they were not at the same depth as before. She had changed. The government was being run by her underlings. The media was turning against her. She was furious.

Spectacular did what she knew to do. She did not consult with you. Nor did she pray to you any longer. So she did what she knew was best for her. She had the power to do it and she did it. She made herself queen. Not a monarch. But a queen of authority that no one in the world had ever had before. A dictator extraordinaire.

She shut up the media and journalists. Only glowing reports about her were allowed to be published or reported. Those who attempted to do differently were jailed. She mandated all her staff and officials follow every letter of her commands. If they did not, they would be replaced immediately.

Spectacular became vindictive. Any who crossed her were dealt with swiftly and with great vengeance. All the people were to worship only her. She spent a great deal of time away from the needs of the country and the people. Fulfilling her longings, desires, and pleasures. Spending money lavishly on herself and those within her inner circle.

The government was running low on money. Spectacular devised a plan. Tax the people. She did. Not just a small tax but a tax of burden. A difficulty for nearly all to pay. Only the extremely wealthy could pay without excruciating difficulty. To make certain the extremely wealthy were subject to her, she gave them the added burden of promoting her and completing favors of every kind.

The people were stunned and overwhelmed. What had happened to Spectacular? This cannot be right. It isn't fair. A few prayed to you for her removal. A few protested. Others longed for her death so there could be a new government. Yet, Spectacular held all the cards, the people had given her complete control. People who publicly spoke against her were imprisoned and some were put to death. Even as they were going to their demise, they pleaded with you not to let them be killed. Their families prayed you would keep them alive, but when you did not, they turned their backs on you. They declared you are an awful god. Not a god anyone can count on.

Those who were enslaved prayed to you for help, for release, for freedom. But it did not come. Spectacular did not relent.

In desperation the people looked away from you with clenched fists and gnashed teeth, spewing venom at you. "Why did you let this happen to us?" "We thought you were god." "A god who loved us and would give us what we wanted."

"Who needs a god like you?" They gave you the proverbial finger, cursed your name, and turned away in disgust. They plan to never speak to you or about you again.

Spectacular remained in complete control.

What are you going to do? You created all of them. Including Spectacular. Do you continue to bless her, even though she has turned away from you? Do you destroy her to please the people she has turned into serfs?

What exactly are you going to do? Do something if you are really god.

You as God

I have blessed Spectacular! I gave her more ability, power, and possessions than nearly anyone else...ever! She has turned into a self-caring, self-fulfilling power monger. It's time to take her out and provide the people a replacement. I will accomplish her demise in such a way that the people will know her death was a direct cause of not following me. Then the people will worship me again. I will send communication so that everyone knows the next leader must be approved by me. You also decided that those who left you or condemned you because life was difficult for a season and not going exactly their way must learn to trust you so that you will see them through. Even though they don't deserve it, I will give them one more opportunity, because I am such a kind God. If they don't shape up, they are going to be plucked out of this world and sent directly to hell...forever!

What the True, Living God Would Do

God requires responsibility of actions. Consequences are a direct derivative of actions. When people follow God and render decisions based upon their faith in God, they will have great consequences (1 John 4:17-19)! A joyful result of actions. They will experience and know God's love. They will adore God and love Him in return for His majestic love. Living and loving even more deeply for God.

For those who utilize their free will for their own benefit a n d do despicable actions there will be bad deplorable consequences (Romans 1:28-32). They will have to deal with and resolve those bad consequences. God will not intervene when they decide to act by their own thought processes (Romans 1:21-23). As long as they are deciding everything on their own and have turned away from God's counsel and guidance, they will experience related results (John 3:18-19).

For Spectacular, she was graced with exceeding abundance and blessings in all facets of her life. She was much given much and God asked for much in return (Luke 12:48). As long as she had a relationship with God she continued to be blessed abundantly. God was honored and glory was given to God for what he had provided Spectacular.

God asks each of us to be His. Since He is Creator God, He calls each of us to lay down our lives and live to serve and honor Him (Mark 12:30).

There are examples in the Bible of the results of turning away from God, worshiping other gods, and living out of relationship, with Him (2 Chronicles 29:6, 8-9). When we focus and live only for ourselves, our pleasures and wants, then we are not delighting in the Lord or His will for us. God gives us guidance on how to live for Him. (Psalm 37:3-6).

If Spectacular would turn back to the Lord God Almighty and ask Jesus Christ (the Son of God) again to be her Savior, she would have a whole new experience. If she repents and asks Jesus to forgive her, she would become a new creature in Christ Jesus (the Son of God) again (Malachi 3:7, 1 John 1:9). While she would still have to live with the consequences of her mistakes, God would be with her and guide her as she walks through the valley of repairing all she had done immorally and ethically wrong. It will not be easy. Yet, since she is again seeking God and His love, she can live a life of joy even in the midst of paying for her actions (John 3:17). No matter what the results. She will have God by her side and His comfort and peace (Psalm 16:11). A peace beyond human understanding. That peace will see her through all things here on earth (John 14:27). She will spend eternity with God (John 10:27-28).

If she denies God and never asks Him into her life again, she will spend eternity separated from God (Galatians 6:8).

1 John 4:17-19 And as we live in God, our love grows more perfect. So we will not be afraid on the Day of Judgment, but we can face him with confidence because we live like Jesus here in this world. 18 Such love has no fear, because perfect love expels all fear. If we are afraid, it is for fear of punishment, and this shows that we have not fully experienced his perfect love. 19 We love each other because he loved us first.

Romans 1:28-32 Since they thought it foolish to acknowledge God, he abandoned them to their foolish thinking and let them do things that should never be done. 29 Their lives became full of every kind of wickedness, sin, greed, hate, envy, murder, quarreling, deception, malicious behavior, and gossip. 30 They are backstabbers, haters of God, insolent, proud, and boastful. They invent new ways of sinning, and they disobey their parents. 31 They refuse to understand, break their promises, are heartless, and have no mercy. 32 They know God's justice requires that those who do these things deserve to die, yet they do them anyway. Worse yet, they encourage others to do them, too.

Romans 1:21-23 Yes, they knew God, but they wouldn't worship him as God or even give him thanks. And they began to think up foolish ideas of what God was like. As a result, their minds became dark and confused. 22 Claiming to be wise, they instead became utter fools. 23 And instead of worshiping the glorious, everliving God, they worshiped idols made to look like mere people and birds and animals and reptiles.

John 3:18-19 There is no judgment against anyone who believes in him. But anyone who does not believe in him has already been judged for not believing in God's one and only Son. 19 And the judgment is based on this fact: God's light came into the world, but people loved the darkness more than the light, for their actions were evil.

Luke 12:48 But someone who does not know, and then does something wrong, will be punished only lightly. When someone has been given much, much will be required in return; and when someone has been entrusted with much, even more will be required.

Mark 12:30 And you must love the Lord your God with all your heart, all your soul, all your mind, and all your strength.

2 Chronicles 29:6, 8-9 Our ancestors were unfaithful and did what was evil in the sight of the Lord our God. They abandoned the Lord and his dwelling place; they turned their backs on him. 8 That is why the Lord's anger has fallen upon Judah and Jerusalem. He has made them an object of dread, horror, and ridicule, as you can see with your own eyes. 9 Because of this, our fathers have been killed in battle, and our sons and daughters and wives have been captured.

Psalm 37:3-6 Trust in the Lord and do good. Then you will live safely in the land and prosper. 4 Take delight in the Lord, and he will give you your heart's desires. 5 Commit everything you do to the Lord. Trust him, and he will help you. 6 He will make your innocence radiate like the dawn, and the justice of your cause will shine like the noonday sun.

Malachi 3:7 Ever since the days of your ancestors, you have scorned my decrees and failed to obey them. Now return to me, and I will return to you, says the Lord of Heaven's Armies.

1 John 1:9 But if we confess our sins to him, he is faithful and just to forgive us our sins and to cleanse us from all wickedness.

John 3:17 God sent his Son into the world not to judge the world, but to save the world through him.

Psalm 16:11 You will show me the way of life, granting me the joy of your presence and the pleasures of living with you forever.

John 14:27 I am leaving you with a gift—peace of mind and heart. And the peace I give is a gift the world cannot give. So don't be troubled or afraid.

John 10:27 My sheep listen to my voice; I know them, and they follow me. **28** I give them eternal life, and they will never perish. No one can snatch them away from me.

Galatians 6:8 Those who live only to satisfy their own sinful nature will harvest decay and death from that sinful nature. But those who live to please the Spirit will harvest everlasting life from the Spirit.

Chapter Five

LIFE ISN'T FAIR

GREG LOVED ASHLEY WITH his whole heart. With his mind and his soul. He immersed himself in Ashley. She was the one. He knew it. He was positive. Her looks, her sense of humor, and her personality captivated Greg. He loved having sex with her. She did love social media more than Greg. He tried to convince himself he didn't care that she loved social media more than him. He loved sports, but she was not involved or interested. So what? She was his dream come true. Things were going great! Greg could not hardly believe how much he loved her. He thought about her all the time. Wherever he went, whatever he did it, was always about Ashley. He thought about her while he was at work. Whenever playing sports, she was in his conscious or subconscious. He built his life around her. Dreaming of the day when they would marry. They were getting along famously. They both had careers, so money was not an issue yet. Greg knew he was spending too much money on Ashley. He poured out his love on her through material gifts. Ashley wholeheartedly enjoyed being spoiled by the gifts. They talked about moving in together. A plan was orchestrated. Ashley needed to sell her house and move in with Greg at his place. He had a nicer home in a little better neighborhood. A perfect place to raise the two children they were planning.

As they got to know each other more intimately, they did have a few knock-down battles. It seems they were not raised culturally or relationally the same. Greg was driven by what he wanted in life. Not necessarily a lot of material possessions but he certainly wanted emotional gratification. He was social but only with a limited crowd. His ideals were based upon morality and ethics. God was in the mix, but not thought of often. Spending time in prayer and praise was only on his mind when things were going poorly. He was extremely success oriented. Any failure was devastating. He really had not experienced failure. He liked work. It was what he was made for. He gave great effort on the job. Partying was of little interest. He did enjoy hanging out with his buddies. They were great fun. He had an occasional beer with the boys.

Ashley was a stunning beauty. She was quite aware of it. Men were always after her. For as long as she could remember. A considerable part of her life was ignoring or deflecting advances. She did not mind that though. She knew she was a babe, and the guys were hot for her. It gave her confidence and delight. It seemed like wherever she went, the workplace, shopping, social events, the theater, men were looking at her. She was well past letting it embarrass her.

Ashley was raised in a broken home. Her father was gone except the rare occasions when he would pick her up for a weekend. Once she was a teen the relationship with her father was strained. They had nothing in common. She stopped going over to his place. Her mother was old-fashioned and demanding. Ashley's mother did not understand what growing up in today's society was like for a beautiful girl. Through the years, Ashley developed and created her own ideals of how life should be and how people should treat her. She was certain and believed fully that she should be treated with utmost respect and appreciation, no matter what she did. It was just how it should be. No matter what she did or how she acted, she was certain she should still be treated as a queen. She offered no apology for her errors or mistakes. No chance of that happening. She was above that.

Between Greg's required life of success and Ashley's unswerving requirement of ultimate respect and utmost attention under all circumstances, they had a few blowout arguments. They did not see eye to eye on Greg working late when Ashley thought they should be together. Greg did not think he should have to apologize for working a little late. He was working for them, anyway. He wondered why Ashley would be upset and expect him to apologize for being late. He reminded her that he was making extra money for them. However, she always responded that he should get a job where he earned a bigger salary so he didn't work overtime. Greg knew he was also working to advance and get promoted so that could happen. He liked his job and did not want to change. He didn't want to go through the challenges of a career change. He wondered why Ashley wasn't happy for him since he was making great upward strides at work. He told Ashley he thought about her all the time, even when working late.

Ashley didn't understand. Greg wasn't treating her right. He should not be working late. He should make enough money working ordinary hours to spoil her and give her all she wanted within a regular forty-hour work week. Anyway, he should be giving her more. Taking her more places. Taking her on vacations and spending more money on her. Lavishing her with gifts and money. Greg wondered how much would be enough. He somehow knew in the back of his mind nothing would ever be enough. She would always have a craving for more.

As time went on, the work issue grew in proportion. Greg thought he should work and did not apologize for it. Ashley grew discontent by having one or two free nights a week. She thought she would start doing other things since Greg wasn't committed to her. She also wondered why Greg didn't remember her beauty and charm. She could get any man she wanted at any time. Ashley started spending time with some workmates. Girls who went out socially on nights Greg worked late. She grew to the point of enjoying that time with the girls. They went different places and did different things but ended up having nightcaps at the same club every time they went out. It grew to be a habit.

Over time, the company Greg worked for slowed a bit and he did not have to work overtime any longer. He thought that he and Ashley would start hanging out on those nights he was now free, but to his utter amazement, Ashley wanted to hang out with her girlfriends, rather than be with him. Greg started hanging out with his buddies. However, Ashley was always on his mind. He wondered, pondered, and almost obsessed over why Ashley did not want to be with him.

Didn't they have life plans? He wondered if this was how married life would be with Ashley. He didn't like it. He wanted her with him, whenever he was free. He couldn't fathom why she did not want that too. He obsessively kept wondering if he had done something wrong. He didn't think so but there must be something. Then it hit him, she must look differently at his overtime hours than he did. He came to the conclusion that she was upset about being left out. That is why she opted out of seeing him once his overtime stopped.

Ashley thought to herself that she would teach Greg for not being with her whenever she wanted to be together. She reminded herself she could have anyone. Why didn't Greg see that or remember that? She reflected on the fact that Greg was cool, and handsome, yet was sure there were other guys just as cool. Some had even more money than Greg. She could get another man in a moment. She was sure. One night when Ashley was out with the girls and Greg was out with the guys, he decided to knock off early. On his way home he thought about Ashley and wanted to be with her. He knew what club the girls hung out in. He decided to head over, surprise her, and have a great finish to the evening. So he did. Upon arriving at the club, he found Ashley and the other girls. He sauntered over and spoke to her. She was not happy to see him. More like angry. Actually, extremely upset. She wanted to know what he was doing there. She wanted to know why he was checking up on her. He tried to explain, that he missed her and just wanted to see her. She did not buy any of it, even though Greg spoke the truth.

Ashley did not ask him to join them. He mumbled a goodbye and sauntered away. He did not know if Ashley said goodbye or not. He went home. He sent her a text trying to explain. Later that night she shot back a text demanding that he never do that again. She had a right to her privacy and he was completely disrespectful. Ashley decided Greg needed to be grateful for any opportunity to see her. She chided him in the text to never track her down again. Blasting him with exclamations that she doesn't report to him. She let him know that it is her life, and she will live it however she thinks is appropriate for her. She said Greg demeaned her in front of her friends by having to see what she was doing.

Greg responded back with an apology and tried to explain again he just missed her and wanted to see her. Ashley did not buy in. They ended the night on a sour note.

From that moment on Greg decided to do as she said, even though he thought she was way over the top. In time, Ashley started spending another night a week going out with the girls. Greg had even more free time on his hands, wishing he and Ashley could be together more. He tried to think of ways to do that. Ashley was unswerving. She said four days a week together was enough. She told him he would have to be happy with that much time.

Greg felt the relationship was slipping away and he wanted Ashley desperately. Everything he did centered on Ashley. His thoughts, his actions, his plans were all about he and Ashley being together for life.

Ashley on the other hand, still loved Greg but was having a great time with the girls at the club. They started dancing with men that were there. Ashley was thrilled with the attention she was getting. Sometimes, she or one of the girls invited men to join them at their table. Those times at the club elevated her self-worth to even greater heights. She was enjoying being wanted by other men. She said to herself this is what Greg gets for not respecting her and giving her what she wants. From now on she will do whatever she wants.

During the next month, their relationship continued on this downward trajectory. Greg wasn't happy about it. Ashley was moving in another direction. They had contentious times as Greg tried to persuade Ashley to spend more time with him. She was adamant she would not. Greg felt that she loved going out with the girls more than being with him. Ashley said he was being ridiculous. Yet she did nothing to prove it differently to Greg.

One Saturday morning, Ashley called Greg and said they needed to talk. Greg asked if he could come over. She said no. Telephone only.

Ashley blurted out that she was pregnant. Greg's head exploded; they had stopped having sex at Ashley's request so they could have unique and special sex after they got married. Greg went ballistic. Bellowing that she can't be pregnant because they weren't having sex. Then immediately it hit him. It was another man's baby. He spewed out words about how could she and what happened to her commitment to him. He wanted to know who the father was. Words came pouring out of his mouth, wanting to know how she could have done that to him after all he had done for her.

Ashley screamed back that either Greg treat her with respect or she was going to hang up. Greg couldn't reckon with that statement and said he couldn't respect her since she was a cheater. For some reason he asked her if she was going to keep the baby. Ashley sneered that she hadn't decided. That was her decision and not his.

Greg hung up, bewildered and crushed.

Greg's mind was completely blown up. His mind was all over the place. Going from one thought to another. Racing. Wondering. Wandering. Within moments he thought to himself, "my life is ruined." He thought of how he had built his entire life around her. He thought of how he did not want to go on. His thoughts really came tumbling out toward God. He knew a real God of love could have stopped her from having sex with another man and she would not be pregnant. A true God would have sent Ashley back to him and been his life-long lover. God could have made Ashley be loyal and faithful. He was sure of it. A real God who cared for the humans he created would have kept them in unison all their days. Finally, he contrived that it was God's fault that all those things happened. He looked to the sky and screamed that he hates God! He shook his fist and gnashed his teeth as he screamed out blasphemies at God. He completed his tirade by shouting that God isn't really a God for the people. If He were a God for the people He would have made everything work out perfectly for him and Ashley.

Ashley hung up the phone, wondering if she really did ever love Greg. He had just acted like a jerk to her. He didn't show her the respect and honor she deserves. Then she remembered she was carrying another man's baby and felt remorse for what she did to Greg. She spoke softer, that she was sorry for hurting Greg so badly. She then realized she truly did love him. Then flipped back to her thinking that it really was Greg's fault this all happened because he ignored her by working overtime. Her final thoughts about it were that every other woman would have done exactly what she did. She turned the page.

Ashley moved on to issues about the baby. Should she have an abortion or keep the baby? She was obsessed with having to make a decision. She wished she didn't have to decide. Couldn't she just have a miscarriage? She had always said she was pro-choice. But now she had a life moving inside of her. She realized she did not want to be a mother. There would be huge responsibilities for years. At least 18 years. She shook her head at the impossibility of that happening. She remembered hearing that pregnancy ravages a woman's body. There would be stretch marks, internal changes, and chemical changes. Ashley wanted no part of any of that.

She couldn't stop thinking of the decision she had to make. Then, she thought of God. Suddenly she expelled such disgust at God. She proclaimed that God could have kept her from getting pregnant. Surely God could see she was just having a little fun. Certainly God would know there is nothing wrong with a little fun. She pronounced that God should have given her a break. She had never done anything against God. Why did he let her get pregnant? She told God that maybe she should have spent more time with God than hanging out at the club, but she was just living a little. She evoked that her whole pregnancy thing was God's fault. She emitted that God just isn't fair. She wanted things to be fair. She suddenly realized that if she had the baby, she wouldn't be able to go out with her girlfriends anymore. She would have to take care of the baby. She looked in the mirror and snarled at God that she hates him.

Ashley couldn't decide what to do. Deliver the baby or abortion. Weeks went by. She could not make up her mind. She had not heard from Greg. She realized she loved him and that he was the one she wanted to spend the rest of her life with. How could she ever expect him to take her back? She prayed to God, saying that if God really loved her, he would bring Greg back and she would have a miscarriage.

Greg meantime, was despondent. Depressed. Ashley was everything to him. He did not know where to go or do or be. His life was totally shaken. Destroyed, in his words. He has no interest in work, or sports, or being with his buddies, or even living. He is immersed in depression. There is one thing he is sure of; it is God's fault. He could have made everything work perfectly just as Greg had dreamed, yet he didn't. He could have. But he wouldn't do it for Greg. Greg again spewed hatred toward God. He asked himself why he is alive. There is nothing for him to live for anymore. If he could die, he would then see God in person and tell him what an awful God he has been to him.

You have watched, listened, and observed. Greg is suffering and Ashley has a decision to make. You have sent your Spirit to be with Greg if only he would open his heart to your Spirit to hear. Finding solace, comfort, and guidance. You sent your Spirit to counsel Ashley about the baby.

You realize that Greg is suicidal and may take his life. You are not calling him to do so. He is despondent and not responding to anything you send from Your Spirit. He is only looking with animosity and hate toward you for not providing the fulfillment he wanted. He is ignoring all the people in his life who have faith in you. He is turning aside, only looking at his pain. He is adamant that you should have fixed the situation so he and Ashley would be together, without a pregnancy involved. He still wants that, yet at the same time is revolted at her infidelity. He wants to hurt her...emotionally. Just like she hurt him.

Ashley, on the other hand, is most appalled and angry with you. She thinks that you should have kept her from getting pregnant. She keeps saying to herself, to you, and to others that she was just having a little fun. She doesn't want to deal with the whole pregnancy thing and is adamant that you fix it by letting her miscarry before she has to get an abortion. She doesn't want the baby and is not interested in being a mother. Not with all the responsibility and requirements of motherhood.

You as God

You ponder what to do. Are you going to let Ashley have a miscarriage? You supposedly are a good God who loves everyone by giving everyone whatever they want. So will you let it happen?

Will you accept Greg's hatred for you and give him what he wants even though he now hates you? If you give him what he wants he will hurt Ashley emotionally. Will you give him that opportunity? Is it acceptable to you? Remember you are a loving God who gives everyone whatever they want. Will Greg ever return to you in faith even if you answer his prayer?

Or will you alter Greg's mind? Will you convert his thought process to again pursue and love Ashley even though she was unfaithful? Are you going to allow Greg to have free will? Or will you decide what is best for him and alter his mind while he sleeps?

Will you be able to keep making decisions based upon the premise that you give everyone everything they want? Even if it is wrong? Even if it is morally unacceptable? Even if others will be harmed emotionally?

Well, what will it be? You are God. You have to decide. They both hate you. What is your decision?

As they both hate you, what will you do? Take them both out and send them to hell for hating you?

Or will you allow Ashley to have a miscarriage? With your great power will you draw her and Greg back together after you let her have a miscarriage? If you bring them back together, will Ashley change her life ambition of financial privilege?

Can Greg stop his obsession with suicide?

Will they come back to you and live for you? Thanking you for bringing them back together? Could it be that even if you do all that for them they will still despise you for allowing them to go through that situation and all the effects that came with it?

Or will you reveal to Ashley that she is carrying a baby of great ability. It is a girl who will have qualities and abilities far advanced and needed. She is a baby girl who will honor and live for you. She has the capacity and capabilities to be a great leader. A leader not only of herself and family, but also for a country. She will have the attributes to change the world. Changing the world and in returning will follow God. The world will become a better place during her lifetime. A faithful global initiative will grow, recognizing, believing, and loving you. Will you mandate that Ashley carry this baby? You can make that happen. You are God.

You have reached a decision. Ashley must carry the baby. Greg needs to get a grip and keep working. There will be another woman. A more appropriate one for him. That is your decision and it is final. Now it is time for both of them to get with it. You cannot be all things to all people in all ways. Not everyone can get everything they want. It is impossible with humans! You have millions of other decisions to make. Time to move on. You have so many things waiting for you.

What God Does

Previously you had instructed and inspired your wise and faithful Prophets to write words called Scripture into a compiled book...The Bible. There is a story in one chapter that speaks to how you will send Christian instructors to show the people how to come to you and enjoy rewards and an inheritance through you.You know some will not see great earthly riches or physical rewards while they live. However, when they come to eternal life in Your Holy Mountain (heaven) they will have an inheritance and rewards forever more, which far exceed anything available on earth.

You decide to send more Instructors that hopefully will influence Greg, Ashley, and others to turn back to you. To make decisions about their circumstances and life. Yet you know many will still not believe in the love and security you provide.

You decide to send the Instructors anyway. Even though they will suffer persecution and rejection. Be defamed and ridiculed. Still you will use this approach, knowing there will be a few who will believe and follow you.

If Greg and Ashley turn to you, seek you, listen to your wise counsel, then you will go to both of them and guide them the rest of their days in all they do. That does not mean there will not be difficulties. Greg will have to live with the loss of his loved one. He will have to grieve her unfaithfulness. He will need to overcome the mountain of his suicidal tendencies. That can all be accomplished by faithfully coming back to you and giving his life totally over to you. You will heal him and make a way as he passes through the emotional waters of difficulty. You will be with him as he walks through the fires of grieving. He will not be burned. You are God and there is nothing you cannot do. God loves Greg and will redeem him and summon him to himself. He will teach Greg that God created him for His glory, (Isaiah 43:1-7). Greg will find purpose to live through God and it will be a life of abundance, beyond Greg's wildest imagination.

God is present with Ashley. He is always near to everyone. He will provide her counsel in her decision about carrying the baby or having a miscarriage if she will turn to Him. God allowed that baby to be formed and created. It is alive in her. Ashley will need to make a decision. Hopefully a decision based upon looking at a much bigger picture than just herself. Can she look past just her own desires and see the opportunities and responsibilities of accepting what she has done? If she turns to the Lord, He will also fully be with her. God will be with her each day to guide her forward. He will do a new thing in her if she turns to the Lord and puts her faith in Him. Living every day for Him. Then God will create a new thing! She will be able to perceive it if she looks beyond her own desires. She will see it springing up. God will make a way in her wilderness and streams in the barren places. He will help her forget the former things and guide her in living a fresh, delightful, rewarding life with Him (Isaiah 43:16-19).

Our God is a forgiving and loving God. He sent God his Son, Jesus Christ, into the world, not to condemn the world but to save the world through Him. That is how much God the Father loves us. He sent His only Son down from heaven and gave each of us the opportunity to turn to Him and believe in Him. Then each one who does will have eternal life with God. No matter what has been done or what has transpired in your past. But you must accept Jesus as your Savior and mean it with your whole mind and heart. Then you will be assured of eternal life with him (John 3:16-17). It is the only way to heaven and eternal life with God (John 14:6). The door to salvation is open to everyone. No matter what you have done in your past.

Isaiah 43:1-7 But now, O Jacob, listen to the Lord who created you. O Israel, the one who formed you says, Do not be afraid, for I have ransomed you. I have called you by name; you are mine. **2** When you go through deep waters, I will be with you. When you go through rivers of difficulty, you will not drown. When you walk through the fire of oppression, you will not be burned up, the flames will not consume you. **3** For I am the Lord, your God, the Holy One of Israel, your Savior. I gave Egypt as a ransom for your freedom; I gave Ethiopia and Sheba in your place. **4** Others were given in exchange for you.

I traded their lives for yours because you are precious to me. You are honored, and I love you. 5 Do not be afraid, for I am with you. I will gather you and your children from east and west. 6 I will say to the north and south, Bring my sons and daughters back to Israel from the distant corners of the earth. 7 Bring all who claim me as their God, for I have made them for my glory. It was I who created them.

Isaiah 43:16-19 I am the Lord, who opened a way through the waters, making a dry path through the sea. 17 I called forth the mighty army of Egypt with all its chariots and horses. I drew them beneath the waves, and they drowned, their lives snuffed out like a smoldering candlewick. 18 But forget all that— it is nothing compared to what I am going to do. 19 For I am about to do something new. See, I have already begun! Do you not see it? I will make a pathway through the wilderness. I will create rivers in the dry wasteland.

John 3:16-17 For this is how God loved the world: He gave[a] his one and only Son, so that everyone who believes in him will not perish but have eternal life. 17 God sent his Son into the world not to judge the world, but to save the world through him.

John 14:6 Jesus told him, I am the way, the truth, and the life. No one can come to the Father except through me.

Chapter Six

LIFE UPSIDE DOWN

PART I

AYANA LOVED HAWI WITH deeply. She looks out her kitchen window and sees the sun slowly rising in the east. She sighs deeply and wonders what is next in her life? Yesterday she went to the clinic and the Dr. confirmed she had AIDS. She will not have long to live. She needs to prepare herself for living out her final time fully and completely.

She looks inward and relives her time with Hawi. She remembers their first encounter. It had been so delightful to her.

One night a few years ago was one of the few occasions she had agreed to go to the club with her girlfriends. She had no expectation, but the unexpected happened. She knew she was not the most beautiful girl. Her friends kept reminding her that she looked good to give her self-confidence. She thought they were the beautiful ones. She thought she was just an average-looking girl. Ayana pondered and wondered about average-looking girls finding men that would treat them like girls of great beauty. Then the average-looking girls would woo them and wow the men. The man would then want them to be the bride of their dreams. Does that really happen, she wondered? Besides, not everyone can look like a beauty queen.

She had not talked to her older brother about going out with her girlfriends. It was the first time she did not seek his approval. He had dictated her life. It was part of the Ethiopian culture that the oldest boy (big brother) could be dictator in a younger sister's life. He could abuse both verbally and physically if he was inclined to do so. It was accepted. That was the case for Ayana. Her brother took great advantage of her. He manipulated her life. Told her what to do and made her do things for him so that he had a life of ease. But not tonight. He had gone away with his friends for a few days. So she went out with her girlfriends. There may be consequences to pay but she doesn't care at the moment.

As she went to the club that night she was not expecting to be hit on, picked up or to find a soulmate. She did make herself look her best and wore the new dress and pumps she had purchased. As she looked in the mirror, she liked what she saw.

That night at the club, things were going as normal, her beautiful friends were getting asked to dance and getting hit on. Guys were buying them drinks. Since Ayana was shy, she stayed in the background and talked to no one but her girlfriends. Nobody asked her to dance and did not buy her a drink. It was turning out to be a normal night at the club. She asked herself why she had come. It was the same as the last time.

The evening wore on and she was ready to go home but she knew better than to ask if her girlfriends were ready to go. Besides, they were on the dance floor having a great time.

A few songs later she noticed a man looking at her. As their eyes met, he looked away. She did too. But a few moments later their eyes locked again, and he slowly started walking toward her. She was excited, scared, and unsure, and definitely d id n ot k now h ow to act.

He sauntered over to her and very quietly said hi and told her his name. He said it way too quietly for her to hear him. She tried to say as nicely as she could that he was speaking too softly. He leaned in a bit and said hello and that his name is Hawi. She responded with the same. Then there was an awkward silence. After what seemed like a long time he managed to ask if she came to the club often. She said no and asked Hawi the same question. He said it was not his first time, but it had been quite a while. They acknowledged they had not seen each other there before.

He asked if he could join her. She was uncomfortable but yet curiously inter-ested so she invited him to sit at her table. Besides, she said to herself, there is no one else at the table.

Time went by and they said a few words, but communication was not fluid or easy. They both were shy and unsure of themselves. Finally, Hawi blurted out the words, asking her to dance. It was a slow song and Ayana wasn't sure she wanted the first dance with him to be a slow song. She pondered, wondering if she said no, would that be the last time he asked her to dance. She said yes.

They slowly walked to the dance floor.

It was obvious they were both inexperienced dancers. Yet it seemed to be enjoyable once they relaxed midway through the song. Ayana and Hawi started enjoying holding on to each other even if they were not experienced dancers. Emotions of pleasure went surging through both of them. As the song ended, they were unsure what to do. Hawi was courageous and asked Ayana to join him at his table. She was excited, yet nervous. She was filled with trepidation, but followed him as he took her hand and guided her to his table.

They did not say much at first as the music was so loud they had to yell to be heard. After a few minutes, Hawi leaned over and started talking directly in her ear. He was consumed with the alluring smell of her perfume. He was captivated. He managed to say he liked being with her, thought she was beautiful and was thankful she was willing to spend time with him. Ayana took it all in. Her head was spinning and her heart was pounding at a pace she could not ever remember before. She had never felt this way about a man before. She never imagined these feelings could erupt so quickly. She slowly leaned over and whispered words of gratitude for what he said. Hawi couldn't hear her, so she tried again. That time he heard her and smiled.

As the night advanced, they exchanged lots of smiles and the shyness of both began to subside. They danced to several fast beat songs. They enjoyed watching each other's moves. They smiled a lot. Hawi wished for another slow song so he could pull Ayana close. His wish was granted. They swayed on the dance floor as the drinks they were having were beginning to take effect. Hawi pulled Ayana close. She did not resist in any way. She welcomed it and voluntarily drew in even closer. Their arms were around each other and their bodies were pressed fully against each other. They hardly moved except for a slight sway. They were consumed in the moment.

As the song was ending, Hawi bent forward and placed a gentle, passionate kiss on Ayana's lips. They both soared to new heights. Such emotion in a touching of lips. Neither would ever be the same. At that moment they both knew they would be together. They knew they had to be.

They returned to their table, gliding along, stepping in synch, happily holding hands. Hawi leaned in and smelled Ayana's perfume again. His senses were on fire. When seated at the table he reached under the table and touched Ayana's leg. She did not push his hand away, but willingly received it. She reached for his hand and delicately, passionately, placed hers on his.

Hawi was thinking. He knew what he wanted. But did Ayana? It had been sometime since he had sex. His wife had died some eight months ago and he had not been with a woman since. He was only 24 and yearned to make love to a woman again. In his opinion it had been far too long. He was unsure how to ask. He stopped speaking for a few minutes as he pondered how he could ask Ayana if she would like to be with him overnight. He wanted sex with her but he also wanted a relationship with her. If it meant waiting as they built their relationship, he was willing.

With his thoughts drawing to an end, Ayana whispered in his ear, asking what was going on with him. So he told her what he had been pondering. She listened and smiled. Hawi wondered what the smile meant. It did not take long for him to find out. She gently took his hand and stroked it lovingly with her hand. Then softly said that she wanted all of that. Hawi looked a little confused. So she said she wanted the relationship and also sex. She wanted it now. But he had to know that she was a 19year-old virgin. Hawi beamed. It was just what he dreamed of. He had never been with a virgin.

He asked if she would like to go to a hotel with him. She said yes. He said he needed to find one on his phone. She was agreeable. It took some 20 minutes of painful searching to find a hotel that was available. He booked the reservation.

Ayana's girlfriends had been watching with glee as they saw what was transpiring. They had made eye contact with Ayana several times and beckoned her to keep going. It was no surprise to them when Hawi and Ayana stood up, put on their coats and headed out. Ayana simply waved goodbye to her girlfriends. They smiled back and clapped their hands in approval.

Hawi and Ayana went to the hotel. The act was consummated. They both thought it was marvelously wonderful. Even after, they could not release each other or stop kissing.

From that time on they were inseparable. In a month, Ayana moved in with Hawi. She was so happy to be out from under her brother's iron fist. He was opposed of course. But he couldn't legally stop her as she was of age.

Ayana's and Hawi's lives together were most enjoyable. Filled with fondness and happiness. Which of course led to deep abiding love. They learned about each other and told their life stories. Ayana was sorry to hear that Hawi was a widower but she was overjoyed he was now hers. She never did ask how she died.

It was only a few short months later that they decided that it would be proper to be married as they were both Orthodox. The event took place as soon as possible. The ceremony brought both deep abiding pleasure and the greatest memories were made. Speaking of memories, their honeymoon was a complete delight. Filled with cherished times together.

That first year together was the thrill of a lifetime. They both wondered how things could ever be better. They were hardly ever in disagreement and were quick to make up. Their way of making up was to head to the bedroom, where making love finalized forgiveness.

At the thirteen-month mark of their marriage, Hawi started realizing he wasn't feeling good. Something was going on inside him. He did not know what was going on or what was happening to him. He tried to hide it from Ayana but she soon caught on. She wanted her groom healed. She demanded he go to the doctor, which he reluctantly did. At the appointment, blood was taken as they were testing for all sorts of possibilities. Both Hawi and Ayana were anxious, but they held on to each other as they waited.

The call came from the doctor two days later that Hawi must come in to discuss the findings. Ayana persisted on going. However, the appointment was at a time when she was to be working. Hawi said he could go alone. He promised to tell her everything. So he went alone.

That night when Ayana came home, she raced to Hawi's side to hear the results. His face gave away deplorable news. A sense of dread came over her. Yet she tried to remain calm. She sat beside him, gently caressing his hand.

He tried to look at her but failed. He blurted out with a broken voice and tears streaming down his cheeks that he had AIDS! The disease was rampant in that part of Ethiopia and they both knew people who lost their lives to it. They knew families that had been torn apart. Life spans were shortened, and loving marriages were destroyed by this disease. It was out of control in Ethiopia and other African countries. There was no answer, no cure. Only death.

Hawi was scared and Ayana joined him. They were both scared for Hawi and also fearful that Ayana may have contracted it.

Ayana braced herself, and conjured up all her courage, asking Hawi if anything could be done for him. He said no, it was too advanced. He did not have a long life ahead of him. It was such devastating, deplorable news that Ayana could only numbly sit by him realizing all their future together had been dashed to the ground. No family, no future, no long joyful life together. Now, just death. She cried uncontrollably.

After a time Hawi said he had to tell her something. She was hardly ready for more news but said okay. He explained to her that his former wife had died of AIDS.

If Ayana had not been struck down before, she was totally overcome now. She wondered why he had not told her. Why would he do that to her? Why did he go to the club and pick her up without being tested for AIDS? Now they were at this point and life looked hopeless. Certainly for Hawi and maybe for herself. She did not know what to do or say.

Ayana became angry, very angry. By morning she was outraged. She could not believe Hawi did not tell her or take precautions. She actually thought that Hawi deserved to die for what he had done to her. It took everything in her not to want to kill him. He had destroyed their marriage and future lives. He was going to die very soon and she might have the disease too. She couldn't bear it. She kicked Hawi out of their bedroom and spent as much time as she could there.

She was not willing to care for Hawi. Let him rot. He deserved it. He had deceived her and there was no way for him to fix any of it. All that was left was his death sentence and probably hers too. She was filled with rage and her wrath was consuming her. She kept wondering what she could do to Hawi for what he had done to her. In her eyes, he was despicable, and she never wanted to see him again. Ayana wanted Hawi out of her life. He had ruined her. Nothing was left for her but to see if she had AIDS and plan out the little time she might have left.

Over and over, she plotted how she could take revenge on Hawi, but she couldn't think of anything other than to murder him. But she couldn't get up the courage to do that. She wanted to kill him. Oh, how she wanted to destroy him. Yet Ayana knew that nothing, absolutely nothing could ever give her back what they had before she found out Hawi had AIDS. Then, of course, she has most likely contracted it herself. Because of Hawi! How she despised him now.

She soon realized she still loved Hawi, but hated that he did not tell her about the AIDS situation. She asked herself if she should stay with him until the end or move on now in an attempt to avoid contracting the life-ending disease.

One day, Ayana flew into a rage and kicked Hawi out of the house. She wanted him dead. But not a death due to AIDS. She wanted to exact death on him. In her way.

She plotted and schemed. Spent hour upon hour thinking of how to murder him. Yet in the end she realized that no matter how she exacted revenge on him, it would not take away the fact that she probably had AIDS and murdering him would never, ever change that. Oh, how she wished there could be a way she could kill Hawi, and it would heal her of potential AIDS.

The day came when she went to the medical clinic to be tested for AIDS. The results were as she expected. She had contracted AIDS. Her life will end in the near future.

A few months later she got the news that Hawi had died. She thought good riddance. She had believed more firmly every day that he deserved to die. He had intentionally given her the disease that was going to take her life. She was incensed that he had deliberately acted to kill her.

Ayana knew she would never forgive him. Never forget what he had done to her. Even though Hawi was dead she would somehow take revenge even if she did not know how she would do it.

She did not know what to do with herself, where to go or whom to be with. Her grieving was overwhelmingly intense. It was intense because of the fury she felt toward Hawi and also knowing how she had given her total love and heart to him. Her mother kept telling her she should move back home. Ayana told her mother she would not if her older brother was still there. He had abused Ayana when she was young. She was surprised to learn her brother had moved to Addis Ababa. She went to live with her mother. Her parents had divorced when she was young. So it was just her mom and younger sister in the house. Her mother cared for her deeply and wonderfully. Yet, taking revenge somehow, someway, on someone was Ayana's sole reason for living. Nothing else mattered anymore.

Ayana went through the stages of grief. Not missing one. Repeating nearly all of them over and again. Yet she would not and could not get over the raging anger she felt toward Hawi. She determined she must somehow re-enter the world. However, she made the promise to herself that she was re-entering the world only to take vengeance on Hawi. He ruined her life. Now she would die young, not have a husband and family. She would never be able to have a husband or see her children grow up and make her a grandmother.

She had somehow kept her job through it all. Some of her coworkers were most kind to her. They kept asking her to go out with them. Ayana had always said no but then unexpectedly one day she said yes to their invitation. She could hardly believe she said yes. She had not gone anywhere or done anything for over a year. Yet, she surprised herself by saying that yes, she would go to the club with her coworkers.

She wondered if her going to the club was destiny. Was it going to be her chance to invoke vengeance toward Hawi onto someone else? She hoped so.

She knew in her mind that if she was ever given the chance, she would deliberately complete her vengeance toward Hawi even if vengeance was deployed onto someone else.

If You Were God

Hawi, before you died, I gave you the verdict that you were going to hell for destroying another person's life just for your pleasure and desires. You said you were religious, so you had to know what my Counsel (your book of instruction) says about harming others for your own benefit. Ayana had every right to kick you out and make you die alone.

Ayana, I am here for you. You don't think of me, or pray to me or consult with my Counsel or see the religious person that is available for you. Come back to me and seek a path for your life after this incredible devastation. I will be with you the entire way.

If you take revenge, be careful on who it will be. I understand completely why you want vengeance. Hawi treated you so deceitfully. Especially after you gave him your love. He deserves life in hell. Be careful and very selective of how you will seek revenge and on who you will live out vengeance. Try not to take anyone's life.

What God Does

Hawi, you must repent of your very wrong way of living with Ayana and confess your sin. You must divulge your sorrow and disgraceful way of life to the priest. Through me he will lead you through the process of repentance and give you instructions of writing a letter to Ayana in which you take all responsibility for all the perverse actions you took.

After that, then if you confess your sins to me, I will forgive you. But you must do more before you leave this earth.

You must change your life habits toward living for me in your few days left. You will have to make video recordings that can be played for all people so they will know your actions. You will need to coach them on how to live for God rather than the way you lived for yourself. Counsel them to go to me, seek me as their Savior, and tell them I can and will help them through all things.

Ayana, revenge is mine. As you know in the Bible, I declared several times that I am the one who seeks vengeance for you. It is not right for you to do so, for I have decided. Taking revenge yourself, will ruin your life. I will do it for you. In a way or ways you will not be able to think of.

Come to me and I will give you rest and comfort. I will love you through the rest of your days on earth and you will leave a marvelous impact on others you communicate with the rest of your life. You can speak to others what it was like to have a husband you loved, who deceived you and is cutting short your life. You will be able to tell how through me, you have found console, comfort, and are able to love in return all those who love you. You will have great impact on helping others to forgive through their newly found Savior, Jesus Christ. You will influence so deeply that many will accept eternal life through Jesus and will spend eternal life with us.

First you must grieve, release, and forgive. I am sending a counselor priest to help you with that. Then take the opportunity to speak to others about your story and how you will be spending eternity in heaven with me.

I know it sounds impossible to forgive and not take revenge, but I will take you through every step. I will constantly be by your side and you will know of my presence. I will carry you through. I will welcome you into heaven on the day you leave earth.

To be continued.

Chapter Seven

LIFE UPSIDE DOWN CONTINUED

BEMNET SAT AT THE table, taking gulps of coffee as he looked out the window. Taking a drag from his cigarette, he refl ects about the last year. He was tormented about his relationship with Ayana. It was spectacular and awful, all in one. Parts of the relationship were incredibly marvelous. Ayana had moments of intense caring and love toward him but most of the time she seemed like she had to fulfill something. It almost seemed like she had to do something heinous and evil. He felt she was convinced she had to do this evil. It was her life goal. Nothing would stand in the way. No matter how much he loved her, he could not break down the wall of evil intent that she was living out. Nothing. It turned out to be an impossible situation. He loved her so very much and he could tell she had feelings for him. However, more than anything else she was consumed with doing something deplorable. In his mind, her love for him was minuscule compared to the monster that was driving her to do evil. If he only knew what it was. That was the question he asked himself hundreds of times. He even went so far as to ask Ayana. But she cast him aside saying that he had no idea what he was talking about.

In some ways he was still dazzled by the memory of meeting Ayana that night at the club. He had been stricken the moment he saw her. His mind leapt with marvelous reverie of that night at the club. He knew he must find a way to meet her. He had had other women before, but none set his heart on fire like Ayana.

She could be the one. He told himself to hang on. Wait a minute, he told himself. I didn't come here to find a relationship or a wife. He wasn't ready for that. He had too much of life to live yet before he became a family man. After all, he was only 27. Sure, someday he wanted to be married and have kids but not yet. He was a football player and played whenever he could. He was not quite good enough to have made the professional teams, but he was on a traveling team that played all over Ethiopia. It paid him a little but not enough to support a family. He knew he would have to give up football to take on a family.

He coached himself about a possible romantic relationship, letting his emotions get ahead of him and thinking long-term thoughts about a woman he does not know. He tried to calm down, but he couldn't. He was stricken. He was throwing down drinks and watching her from a distance. He wasn't talking much with his friends and not asking anyone to dance. His friends were surprised and wondered what was wrong with him. He told them he just needed to sort a couple things out in his mind. He said he was okay and that they should keep doing their thing.

As he watched Ayana, he noticed she wasn't talking much with the friends. She was only sipping a drink and wasn't dancing. Why wasn't she being asked to dance? Why? She was gorgeous in his mind. Bemnet started to wonder if it was destiny that she was being reserved that night for him. He had to chuckle at that thought.

He was amazed that he did not have the courage to go ask Ayana to dance. He had asked hundreds of others to dance in the past and had great success. But this time he wanted to succeed very badly, yet the possibility of her saying no was hounding him.

After a time, his buddies saw him looking over in that direction and goaded him, saying that he had to go for it. They persisted. He slowly rose and began walking her way. His buddies applauded as he went. He gave them the universal sign as he got going.

Slowly he ambled over to Ayana. She had not noticed him. He slowly came to her, standing close but not too close. He told her his name, saying that he had noticed her and wondered if she would like to dance. Then he said that he was sorry he did not have a pickup line. They both laughed at that. She said yes, even though she was filled with trepidation. Ayana kept reminding herself of what she came to do. But she couldn't stop thinking that this was a terrific looking young man who was showing interest in her. She was on a mission and must conclude it. She must entice him if she was to fulfill the pact she had made to herself.

Naturally it was a slow song. Bemnet was a gentleman and did not try to pull her close. He realized she could dance. He could too. Ayana thought of how she and Hawi had taken dance lessons after they got together. She was not very comfortable dancing with someone other than Hawi, but she knew she had to keep going forward. Bemnet and Ayana danced several dances. They both found them enjoyable. Before the night ended, he got her phone number.

Slowly a relationship formed. He was gone a lot, playing football. Ayana was thankful as she wasn't ready to dive into another relationship. The relationship grew over time and they eventually fell in love. At least that was what Bemnet surmised. Ayana found herself caring for Bemnet but that was always overruled by her mission of vengeance.

Bemnet was not yet ready to give up his life of football. He knew he couldn't be the provider he needed to be while playing football. So they just kept dating. They started having sex. Bemnet fell deeply in love with Ayana. She loved the sex.

Ayana told him she was a widow and that her former husband had a long-term illness, but didn't share that Hawi died of AIDS.

Bemnet didn't ask and she didn't tell.

Months into their relationship Ayana began feeling different, like ill. She didn't know how to explain it. Something wasn't right. She went to the doctor and he told her she was entering into another stage of AIDS. She was not surprised. But what was she to do?

In the following days, she realized she had an even greater hatred toward Hawi who gave her AIDS and did not reveal it to her. She was still livid with anger at what he had done to her. Now she had full-blown AIDS and she continued to seethe with rage against him. She was going to die and nothing could stop it. She was too young. There is no way she should be dying this early in life. Somebody had to pay for what Hawi did to her. The one who was going to pay was Bemnet.

She decided she would coerce Bemnet into marrying her. They continued to have sex and it was fun. She might as well have as much sex as possible before she died. Occasionally she thought of what she was deliberately doing to Bemnet. She was always able to overcome that brief feeling of guilt by remembering what Hawi did to her. Besides, it was the only happiness she experienced with death looming.

Her life was all mixed up. A small part of her wanted to be loved in her final time on earth, but her never-ending mission was to take revenge on Hawi by giving AIDS to another person. She thought, who could blame her, she was treated dirty by Hawi. She drove a stake in the ground telling herself over and over she would not tell Bemnet about her AIDS condition. She decided to come on stronger to Bemnet and advance marriage immediately. He was keen on the idea except for giving up football, which didn't provide enough income.

Ayana talked to her mom and got approval to have them move in for a time until Bemnet's football career ended. But after that he must get a job and they must go. Ayana relayed that to Bemnet. After a few days he came to accept the idea. He loved Ayana and football. It seemed like a decent compromise. They proceeded forward.

There was a lovely wedding service with family and a few friends. The honeymoon was only a weekend getaway as they did not have much money.

Life in Ayana's mom's house was okay. Bemnet was gone a lot, playing football. Ayana enjoyed having her mom coddle her. But she could not tell her mom she had AIDS.

When Bemnet returned from matches, he couldn't wait to get his hands on Ayana. She complied. She had a sexual hunger. Unfortunately, Ayana's health was beginning to deteriorate. For some unexplainable reason she had decided not to take birth control. She thought the pills might make her condition worse. Soon she discovered she was pregnant.

Ayana still wanted revenge against Hawi. Yet there came a time she became plagued with thoughts of what she was doing to Bemnet and the baby. Most likely they would both contract AIDS from her. Their lives would end early because of what she gave them. While it made her feel somewhat bad, it was a very small consideration compared to the overwhelming revenge she wanted against Hawi. Nothing would overcome the rage she felt toward Hawi.

Ayana could tell her health was declining. With her physical and emotional health deteriorating, she wondered if she could keep the AIDS secret until her death. She also wondered if the baby would die with her before delivery. If so, that was fine with her. It was no big deal to her. The child was going to have AIDS anyway and die a very early death.

While Bemnet was ecstatic about the news about a baby, he did not know how he could support his family while still playing football. The matches brought him an exhilarating high. Highs only exceeded by the thought of being a husband and father. He spent a great amount of time thinking of ending his football career and finding a job so he could be home with Ayana and their future daughter. He told Ayana he was going to quit football, stay home, and be a good provider. Ayana could not have cared less but said that it was a good plan. Even after he quit football and found a job, he fully immersed himself into his new life as husband and future father. He did not spend futile time looking back at his lost football career. He had a new season of life and he embraced it fully.

Ayana continued through the terms of pregnancy without having to reveal her condition to anyone. Of course, her doctor knew.

But no one else.

Delivery time arrived during the middle of the night. Bemnet just shook his head and smiled that of course it had to happen during the middle of the night. Off to the hospital they went. Delivery was a very excruciating experience for Ayana. She had little strength but somehow brought her baby into the world. A beautiful child of God.

Bemnet beamed with joy but was also concerned about Ayana and how poorly she was doing. He kept caressing her hair and telling her how much he loved her, as the baby girl was laid upon her chest, he gently stroked the baby to calm her crying.

The Dr. stepped in and congratulated them. He patted Ayana and said that she did so well in delivery even though she had AIDS.

Ayana could not stop his words before they were said. She moaned and glanced at Bemnet, who was in compete shock. Bemnet said to her, "You have AIDS." He didn't say it just once or twice, but at least ten times. Maybe more. He slouched into a chair close by. Both of his hands cradled his head as he shook it back and forth repeatedly. Ayana heard him say that it just had be. He thought she should have told me earlier. Then he would have done everything possible to save her. Bemnet whispered, "What can I do for her now? Is there anything?"

Ayana broke down and wailed in agony. Not agony for what she had done. But in agony that her life was about to end and it was all because of what Hawi did to her. There was also a sense of accomplishment that she had successfully achieved her vengeance.

Ayana's life of motherhood ended within a few months. She and Bemnet did not resolve things in any fashion. He cared for the baby. She did not. She died alone. Satisfied that she had succeeded in her mission.

The baby awakens and cries. Bemnet puts down his coffee cup and gathers up his daughter. The daughter of his dreams. But his dream is only partially fulfilled and will never totally come true. His love for Ayana continued even after the life-shattering news right after their daughter's delivery.

Bemnet doesn't know how he will carry on as a single father. A baby to care for that takes many, many hours a day and he must find a way to financially support both of them. He wants to provide a wonderful life for his daughter. But how? He doesn't know how. Even more overwhelming was the undeniable fact that both he and his daughter had contracted AIDS. They would both die soon.

He turns to God and pleads for a way and means to make it all work out.

If You Were God

Ayana, you got your revenge. I can see why you wanted it and thought you deserved it. It was awful how Hawi left you with nothing but to carry AIDS and face a premature death. You left me behind once you found Bemnet and made him the source of your revenge. Was it the right type of revenge? Didn't you just repeat what Hawi did to you?

The last part of your life you lived totally away from me and my counsel. You did not turn to me once, even on death's door. You did not want me at the end because I let Hawi give you AIDS. Since you left me behind, how can I accept you to live eternally with me? I can't.

Bemnet, you weren't listening to me. I was telling you to not get involved with her. Why weren't you seeking me out? Living for me? Why was living your own way so important to you? Leaving me in the dust. Now look at what happened because you went on your own without seeking my counsel. I have half a notion to leave you on your own again and let you go directly to hell after you die. You are in such a mess. I had the answer for you. The answer of not to date Ayana, but you would not listen. No, not you. You had to go it alone without my wisdom and direction. I can't believe you got yourself into such a predicament. I am contemplating. Do I leave you all alone and make myself unavailable to you for the rest of eternity or give you a break and live with you? I have to think about it. If I had to decide at this moment, I would leave you forever. However, I am not going to consider the matter more fully. Or Who knows, maybe I will decide to make myself available to you again? I don't know right now. I need time to think. It is not an easy decision. I have so many things to do and decisions to make for millions of others. I don't know. I will give it some thought. I will get back with you. Maybe I will have time to decide in the next five to ten years. Suck it up and do what you can until I get back with you. You're a father. Get on with it.

By the way, it is a bummer what Ayana did to you. I sent her directly to hell.

What God Does

Bemnet, my son, I love you. I will always be with you. Life has dealt you heavy blows. Not many people could have stood during what you have experienced. The pain and blows would have been too heavy for most others. I am here for you. I am your God and you have leaned into me. I love you. For you are a child that I created who turned to me in your darkest hour. I am sending my Holy Spirit to you, over and over, again and again. Every day. Listen for his counsel, divine guidance, and comfort (John 14:26).

I will never leave you. I will not fail you or abandon you (Joshua 1:5b). I will make a way through this wilderness and provide refreshment in your dry and thirsty land (Isaiah 40:3).

I will protect you and carry you gently and carefully as you care for your daughter (Isaiah 40:11). I will be your counsel and I will speak to you and sing over you (Psalm 73:24, Zephaniah 3:17).

When you do not know what to do, I will be with you to provide answers for all things (Psalm 121:2). I will guide you in building a firm foundation of faith so it may be well with you and your daughter even when life is terribly hard (Matthew 7:24-27).

Lead your life in love for me and others. Raise your daughter to come to me (Deut. 4:9). I will fill you with wisdom and wisdom will be your partner and good counsel all your days, no matter what comes (Proverbs 2:1-6).

My love abounds for you forever (Psalm 136:2).

Ayana did not turn from her evil ways. Even in her final days she denied me as her God. She cursed me and told me she would never follow me because of what I let Hawi do to her. When she came before me after her death, she still seethed in anger against me and told me she wanted nothing to do with me. Not now, not ever.

All will be judged for their actions on earth (Romans 2:5-6). Believers have been forgiven their sins and enter heaven (1 John 4:17). Those who reject Jesus Our Savior will be judged for not believing in Him (2 Corinthians 5:10). Jesus Christ cannot let anyone who hates him live in heaven with him and with those that love Jesus (Revelation 20:11-12). Jesus honored Ayana's wish. She will spend eternity in hell (Romans 1: 28-32 CEV).

John 14:26 But when the Father sends the Advocate as my representative—that is, the Holy Spirit—he will teach you everything and will remind you of everything I have told you.

Joshua 1:5b For I will be with you as I was with Moses. I will not fail you or abandon you.

Isaiah 40:3 Listen! It's the voice of someone shouting, Clear the way through the wilderness for the Lord! Make a straight highway through the wasteland for our God!

Isaiah 40:11 He will feed his flock like a shepherd. He will carry the lambs in his arms, holding them close to his heart. He will gently lead the mother sheep with their young.

Psalm 37:24 Though they stumble, they will never fall, for the Lord holds them by the hand.

Zephaniah 3:17 For the Lord your God is living among you. He is a mighty savior. He will take delight in you with gladness. With his love, he will calm all your fears. He will rejoice over you with joyful songs.

Psalm 121:2 My help comes from the Lord, who made heaven and earth!

Matthew 7:24-27 Anyone who listens to my teaching and follows it is wise, like a person who builds a house on solid rock. 25 Though the rain comes in torrents and the floodwaters rise and the winds beat against that house, it won't collapse because it is built on bedrock. 26 But anyone who hears my teaching and doesn't obey it is foolish, like a person who builds a house on sand. 27 When the rains and floods come and the winds beat against that house, it will collapse with a mighty crash.

Deuteronomy 4:9 But watch out! Be careful never to forget what you yourself have seen. Do not let these memories escape from your mind as long as you live! And be sure to pass them on to your children and grandchildren.

Proverbs 2:1-6 My child, listen to what I say, and treasure my commands. 2 Tune your ears to wisdom, and concentrate on understanding. 3 Cry out for insight, and ask for understanding. 4 Search for them as you would for silver; seek them like hidden treasures. 5 Then you will understand what it means to fear the Lord, and you will gain knowledge of God. 6 For the Lord grants wisdom! From his mouth come knowledge and understanding.

Psalm 136:2 Give thanks to the God of gods. His faithful love endures forever.

Romans 2:5-6 But because you are stubborn and refuse to turn from your sin, you are storing up terrible punishment for yourself. For a day of anger is coming, when God's righteous judgment will be revealed. 6 He will judge everyone according to what they have done.

1. **John 4:17** And as we live in God, our love grows more perfect. So we will not be afraid on the Day of Judgment, but we can face him with confidence because we live like Jesus here in this world.

2. **Corinthians 5:10** For we must all stand before Christ to be judged. We will each receive whatever we deserve for the good or evil we have done in this earthly body.

Revelation 20:11-12 And I saw a great white throne and the one sitting on it. The earth and sky fled from his presence, but they found no place to hide. 12 I saw the dead, both great and small, standing before God's throne. And the books were opened, including the Book of Life. And the dead were judged according to what they had done, as recorded in the books.

Romans 1:28-32 Since these people refused even to think about God, he let their useless minds rule over them. That's why they do all sorts of indecent things. 29 They are evil, wicked, and greedy, as well as mean in every possible way. They want what others have, and they murder, argue, cheat, and are hard to get along with. They gossip. 30 Say cruel things about others and hate God. They are proud, conceited, and boastful, always thinking up new ways to do evil. These people don't respect their parents. 31 They are stupid, unreliable, and don't have any love or pity for others. 32 They know God has said that anyone who acts this way deserves to die. But they keep on doing evil things, and they even encourage others to do them.

Chapter Eight

CHARLOTTE'S STARTUP

CHARLOTTE IS AN ENTREPRENEUR. She is gratified, that she had undertaken starting her own business. The small business she started was now holding its own. She had always wanted to start her own business. People told her that her clothing designs for working women were functional, unappealing, and deliberately without sexual appeal. She also thought women should not distract anyone by being sexually alluring at work. Work is work and no time for anything else. Many told her nobody would buy her line of clothes. They were not the latest style and women want to dress seductively. Charlotte was old-fashioned. She somehow knew that companies that had a strong work ethic would value the line. After research and market testing, she found there was a market for her fashion line. Not a market as big as seductive clothes, but they were marketed to women who wanted to attract a sexual partner. So she went for it and started having the line manufactured. She had to slug it out. There were many, many long days and short nights. Time with her husband was compromised. Brandon said he understood since it was going to be their path to financial independence and an early retirement. He was supportive at the start. Yet he did not realize or have a concept of how long it would take for the products to be designed, engineered, and then manufactured. He wondered what all the talk about a patent meant anyway.

Over time Brandon grew frustrated with all the time Charlotte was away from him. They no longer did things together like the days when she was employed full-time. Now Charlotte was working a part-time job and spending many hours a week to get the business off the ground. She worked all day at her own business and worked evenings in the makeup department at Nordstrom. That job certainly didn't pay much. But at least she still had some income. Brandon maintained his job as an ambulance driver for the local city. That was his job for now. He earned money for Charlotte and himself so they would have the needed medical insurance. Brandon did stop adding to his 403(b)plan. Charlotte had used her 401(k) balance for the business. They had to pay a good chunk of that money to the IRS and state for what they called an early withdrawal penalty. Who knew that?

Brandon was hurt, pained, and lonely, yet held on to the bond of marriage between him and Charlotte. Many times, he thought that this valley was deep and getting deeper with no way out. This valley of their marriage was taking a toll. When would Charlotte get the startup going? He wanted to tell her to get it going. To make some money or go back to her old career. He was nearly at the end of his patience. He was very lonely and alone. Yet, he was still hanging in there. They had made a decision for life.

Over the months, his loneliness led him to social websites. He developed friendships with people throughout the country and the world. He told Charlotte about sites and chats he had. She was happy he found something to do while she was working so many hours. She kept telling herself that she would make it up to Brandon just as soon as the business was making money and could pay her a salary. She would quit her job at Nordstrom and they would have more time together. Making up for the lost time. Time for clothing line development drug on and on. Manufacturing delays had kept the business from opening as soon as expected.

Each day, Charlotte's frustration with the manufacturer grew more intense. Charlotte was not high on the totem pole with the manufacturer. She had to wait her turn on the bottom rung. The day finally did arrive when the manufacturer called and said the samples were ready. Charlotte went to the warehouse and picked up a few samples to test. To her disgust she found that her products were made haphazardly and were produced at an inferior grade. She was livid! She knew she could not sell those products. She also knew that she needed this manufacturer. It was the only one who would work with her as a startup. She got no payment terms. She had to pay 40% up front and the remainder at completion. She did get them to agree that she could test the clothes before final payment. Now she had tested them and recognized the inferiority. She knew she could not just call them up and blow them away for inferior and ridiculous work. So, she called the sales rep and asked for a meeting with him and the production supervisor. The sales rep was surprised and nearly offended, but he did agree to the meeting.

The next day Charlotte took the clothes she had tested and went to the meeting. She spoke calmly and rationally, describing the problems. The sales rep was beside himself that production would do such inferior work. He let the production supervisor have it. Several shots were even below the belt. The production supervisor tried to take the news as civilly as possible. After thinking for a moment, he said they would remanufacture the products at no further cost to Charlotte. He also said they would make it a priority.

Charlotte was almost afraid to ask how long it would take. When the production supervisor said two weeks, she almost came undone. She wanted to say lots of negative things. Somehow, she kept her cool and asked if there was any way to get them done quicker. The production supervisor told her that they had to order more of the specialized fabric she wanted for the clothes before they could produce the clothes again. That would take at least a week.

The two weeks could not have passed more slowly. Each day was an emotionally charged uphill battle for Charlotte. She somehow made it through without losing her cool at work and also at home.

Brandon did not take the delay well. He had waited and waited. He thought that once the products were acceptable to Charlotte she would be on her way. But now there is another delay. The two weeks could have been a decade. He was nearly at a breaking point. He wanted Charlotte back and the life they had together, before she started with this crazy idea about a business of her own. He thought they had a great life together before the startup. Now all of Charlotte's retirement was gone, their savings account was nearly exhausted and still she was making nothing. Not a penny.

Charlotte was so anxious to get her business underway. There was a goal not only for financial success for the business but also for Brandon and her. A goal of theirs was to have a baby as soon as Brandon could quit his job. He would be a stay-at-home dad. That meant Charlotte had to make the business successful. The sooner the better. They both knew Charlotte was not getting any younger and carrying a baby full term at her age, while working full time, may be risky.

The newly manufactured product line was produced well and met all of Charlotte's expectations. Now she was ready to market and sell her conservative-minded, work-oriented line of clothes. She initiated the marketing and advertising plans that appealed to professional women of all ages. She was appealing to them to go to work to do work and not try to allure others to them. Saying that work is work and it should be done without interference, especially through the clothes they wear. Then they can strive more easily for success and advancement.

It certainly wasn't a mainstream approach.

Initially sales were slow, which she expected. After several months, sales increased to the level that she gained status at Amazon and now she was rolling. Shopify wasn't doing a lot of volume but it was worth having the option in place. Her contracted sales executives started having success, getting several major chains to carry the line of clothes. She was happy. Things were taking off.

After seven months, Charlotte realized that she has made sufficient income to quit her part-time job. She looked in the mirror and said to herself with a nod, "They said a simple, conservative, well-tailored clothes line would never be successful, but now look at my business." She couldn't help but wink at herself in the mirror.

The next morning Brandon gave a passing kiss and hug as he headed out the door. Charlotte wanted to tell him the good news but he was in a rush to get to work on time. She would tell him that night.

Charlotte was thinking she should plan something special.

Charlotte headed to work with the good news still bringing her joy. Over the last month Brandon had become more and more infatuated with social media. He had many contacts. Every day he was messaging and video calling people he had met. Both female and male. Over time he struck up ever-deepening friendships with both women and men.

Brandon was finding it hard to not continually communicate with Ella. He found they had a great deal in common and enjoyed many of the same things.

Brandon started thinking and fantasizing about her a great deal. They were messaging each other every day. He was surprised and pleased to find that Ella lived in their city. How could it be that Ella also lived in Milwaukee? She lived just 25 minutes away. They talked about meeting up. Then they did. Followed by several more meetings. The talks were intimate and lustful.

At work that day, Charlotte was overcome with happiness as she looked at yesterday's sales. Results indicated another day of record sales. Wow! That was amazing! She started calculating how much time she needed before she would be making enough money to let Brandon quit working. Then they could work on having their dream come true. Having a baby would make their dreams and life together complete. She was so in love with Brandon. She was overjoyed they were together.

As Charlotte was working, she kept thinking about how to surprise Brandon with the good news that she could quit her part-time job and that the business was really making great strides forward. She decided she was going to take off early, pick up a bottle of Brandon's favorite wine, and head home to clean the house before Brandon got home. She had not helped around the house in any way since the business took off. Yup, that was her plan. She would help out at home. She would clean the house, which she hadn't done for over a year. She had left it all up to Brandon. While sitting at her desk, she pondered what had inspired her to think of cleaning the house. It made no sense to her. She never thought of doing that. It was certainly not on her hit parade.

Shortly after lunch, she went to the wine store and bought that special wine Brandon loved. Then she headed home to start cleaning.

Upon her arrival at home, she put the bottle of wine and their best wine glasses on the island counter. She was going to dress up for him tonight and invite him to make extraordinarily marvelous love with her.

Now wait, she told herself, doing the household chores must come first. Then she looked at the sink. There was the first chore to accomplish. It looked like the dishes had been there for several days and the dishwasher was full of clean dishes that needed to be put away. She set to work and got the dishes washed, wiped, and put away. As she finished putting the dishes away that were in the dishwasher, she felt the contentment of accomplishment. She walked into the living room and for the first time in months, maybe over a year, she noticed a thick layer of dust on the furniture. She decided all rooms needed to be dusted and vacuumed. She set to work, starting off with dusting. As she got to the master bedroom, she thought of how the good news would induce them both to make love. It had been a while. She had been so tired lately and Brandon was either sleeping or not in the mood by the time she got home from work. She missed making love a great deal. She sensed Brandon did too. As she thought about it, she wondered if this might be the night he would be open to a little more adventure. He had always been so conservative in the bedroom.

One year she had surprised him with wrist and ankle cuffs to add to their pleasure. Brandon had shrieked when he saw them and said no way. They were still in her night stand and had not ever been put into service.

As Charlotte went to Brandon's side of the bed, she was humming the song they called "their song." As she dusted, she kept thinking about making love with Brandon. As she was stooping over the nightstand, she saw a little box that was just visible under the corner of the bed. She leaned down and stretched to get the box so she could throw it away. She wondered what it was. As she pulled it out, she could tell the box was empty. She had to see what it was. She read the label. It was a sex toy. She said out loud, "What in the world is this?" She looked again. Then again. Yes, she read the box correctly. The box was empty. She sighed out loud, maybe Brandon was starting to come out of his shell. Could this be the night they did something very special in bed? However, she also thought that she should not let her mind get ahead of herself. She reminded herself that Brandon was ultra conservative in bed. She wondered if he would be surprising her with this. She wanted to find that toy. She pulled open his nightstand drawers but nothing was there. She searched through his dresser but nothing there either. Charlotte was on a mission to find it. She wanted them to use it that night. She looked in his bathroom drawers and medicine cabinet. She looked through his travel kit. But she couldn't find it. It slowly came to her. Wait a minute, this sex toy wasn't for her. It was for another woman.

She slumped to the floor. Her head banged against the bathroom wall. She shook her head over and over. Thumping her head against the bathroom wall. How could he? They had their lives planned together forever. They promised they would never be unfaithful. But now it must be, it had to be that Brandon is unfaithful. Yes, it had to be. It was incredibly hard for Charlotte to accept it. Charlotte thought that with all his alone time, he must have sought out another woman. How could he? She was doing all this business stuff for them.

Suddenly she felt enraged. Between clenched teeth she screamed "Wait until he gets home, he is going to get it." But then she wondered what was it she was going to give to him. She quickly thought it through and decided hastily that she would never, ever want him as her husband again. That was it. It is over. No more for him. I am not sharing him. Goodbye Brandon. He will have to leave their house tonight. He wants that other woman. Go to her. He can have her. Charlotte was done with him.

Just like that.

Her mind raced and screamed with what to do. How does she get a divorce attorney and save her business from having to share her business equity with him? She doesn't know any divorce attorneys. But she has seen plenty of ads for them. She would start calling in the morning.

Yet suddenly, she felt alone. Alone and lonely. Who would be there for her? No one. She hated that thought. It exacerbated into hate for Brandon. How could he? After all she had done for him? Now she was the one who was going to be the one left behind and all alone. Charlotte was incredulous.

Her mind propelled through all sorts of things. Then she turned her attention to God,, Charlotte was damning God for letting this happen and saying how she knew she was right for never believing in him. As she was concluding condemning God, she heard the garage door open.

If You Were God

Well Charlotte, look what a fine mess you have gotten yourself into. You have disgraced me and did not believe in me all these years. Going your own way and turning in any direction you wanted to go without seeking my counsel. I did not matter to you as you thought you could do it all. You considered yourself to be better than me. You decided you were God and I should just get out of your way. So look at what an unbelievably painful life journey you are going to go on now. All by yourself, without Brandon or me. You have disgust for him and have damned me. Looks like you don't need me.

I sent signals to you and opportunities for you to recognize the good I was giving to you, even though you were thinking it was just you and your amazing cerebral resources. It wasn't. Some of those things were directly from me. Do you remember how you were overcome with joy that Brandon would actually date you, then get serious, fall in love with you, and marry you? I was in the midst of all that. I was there for him and also there for you if you would have turned to me. It would have been outrageously more wonderful if you had brought me into your love affair. But you didn't. You thought you had it together and knew the plan.

As I see it, things were progressing pretty well until you got the idiotic notion to start a business without Brandon's complete agreement and support. Yes, he said he supported you but he had no idea it meant you would be gone nearly every waking moment for over a year. Then when you did get home, you immediately ate and slept. You weren't even inquiring as to how your spouse was doing or feeling? That is no way to treat a husband, nor could anyone expect him to stay committed to you. Seems like you are fortunate he stayed with you this long. I have seen many other times where men jumped ship much sooner than Brandon did.

So here is my final proposition for you. You certainly don't deserve one. You have been ridiculous.Y ou talk about being young for your age.

That is you. Young all right. You lack knowledge and understanding.

Wisdom is not even in the picture.

Okay, so if you turn to me now, I will help guide you through this mess you have created. There will be dark days and difficult times, but I will see you through. Brandon won't be coming back so you need me more than ever.

I will help make your business successful and will introduce you to a man who follows me.

I will do this if and only if you continue to become my servant and remain so all of your days, starting immediately.

That's it. That is all I have to offer. Take it or leave it. Yu have only a couple of days to decide.

As you are pondering and wondering about what will happen to Brandon, know that he will have severe repercussions for not living for me, destroying the marriage you and he had, and also for ending the marriage of his newfound lover.

What God Will Do

Charlotte, my daughter, come to me. I am your God. Jesus, my son, can be your Savior. When it seems that all is lost, we are here for you. My Spirit, the Holy Spirit,will be constantly with you to guide you and lead you through the upcoming turmoil, pain, and grieving. He will supply you with my love, which is far superior to what any human can provide.

I created you from the depths of my love (Psalm 139:13-18, Jeremiah 1:5). Of course, it does not please me that you have turned your back on me all your life and even cursed me at times. You made fun of me and the people who love me. However, because of my great love for you, I sent my one and only Son (Jesus Christ) to earth to pay for your sins through death on a cross and provided a means to eternal life through Him (Romans 5:8).

You went your own way and accepted the successes you could personally achieve. Now you are facing a great defeat due to the work of your own hands. I gave you over to your own way of thinking because you abandoned me. You left me and followed the god of Charlotte. You left me, the one who is the eternal, all powerful God, so you could direct your life by yourself (Romans 1:22-23, 25). Now you are left to your own demise. Yet, if you turn to me and bend your knee to my Son, and ask Him to beY our Savior, he will certainly become that (Romans 10:9).

You will have to face the results of things you did on earth. Brandon will also. Ultimately, it was his decision to be unfaithful. He could have set a time and talked with you about him needing you in his life. But he didn't. That does not leave you off the hook. You had marital responsibilities that you ignored. You must learn from those mistakes so you will never let them happen again if you find another man.

Come to me and allow me to lead you through life. I am a forgiving God who will forgive you. All you have to do is come to me and ask my Son, Jesus Christ, to be Your Savior. Your sins will be forgiven and your life can start down a new path of love, grace, mercy, and deep relationship. I will always be with you.

Once you come to me with your broken heart and abide in me, I am able and will help you start over and build a new life that will honor both me and you. If you stay with me and surround yourself with likeminded believers, you will be restored and your life will take on a new meaning. A joy will overcome you that you have never known before (2 Cor. 1:4).

The opposite will hold true also, if you do not come to me, believe in me, and follow me; then ultimately, I will do the same to you. If you forsake me, I will eventually forsake you (1 Chronicles 28:9). If you are ashamed of me, I will be ashamed of you (Mark 8:38).

Ultimately, I am a loving and righteous God forgiving all who ask to be forgiven of their sins and seek me as their Savior. When you repent of your ways and live in relationship with me, dedicated to serving me, I will love you and restore you. As you believe in me, I am there for you and with you through all the world puts before you. I can and will help you through all things (Matt. 11:28-30).

Psalm 139:13-18 You made all the delicate, inner parts of my body and knit me together in my mother's womb. 14 Thank you for making me so wonderfully complex! Your workmanship is marvelous— how well I know it. 15 You watched me as I was being formed in utter seclusion, as I was woven together in the dark of the womb. 16 You saw me before I was born. Every day of my life was recorded in your book. Every moment was laid out before a single day had passed. 17 How precious are your thoughts about me, O God. They cannot be numbered! 18 I can't even count them; they outnumber the grains of sand! And when I wake up, you are still with me!

Jeremiah 1:5 I knew you before I formed you in your mother's womb. Before you were born, I set you apart and appointed you as my prophet to the nations.

Romans 5:8 But God showed his great love for us by sending Christ to die for us while we were still sinners.

Romans 1:22-23, 25 Claiming to be wise, they instead became utter fools. 23 And instead of worshiping the glorious, ever-living God, they worshiped idols made to look like mere people and birds and animals and reptiles. 25 They traded the truth about God for a lie. So they worshiped and served the things God created instead of the Creator himself, who is worthy of eternal praise! Amen.

Romans 10:9 If you openly declare that Jesus is Lord and believe in your heart that God raised him from the dead, you will be saved.

2 Corinthians 1:4 He comforts us in all our troubles so that we can comfort others. When they are troubled, we will be able to give them the same comfort God has given us.

1 Chronicles 28:9 And Solomon, my son, learn to know the God of your ancestors intimately. Worship and serve him with your whole heart and a willing mind. For the Lord sees every heart and knows every plan and thought. If you seek him, you will find him. But if you forsake him, he will reject you forever.

Mark 8:38 If anyone is ashamed of me and my message in these adulterous and sinful days, the Son of Man will be ashamed of that person when he returns in the glory of his Father with the holy angels."

Matthew 11:28-30 Then Jesus said, Come to me, all of you who are weary and carry heavy burdens, and I will give you rest. 29 Take my yoke upon you. Let me teach you, because I am humble and gentle at heart, and you will find rest for your souls. 30 For my yoke is easy to bear, and the burden I give you is light.

Chapter Nine

DR. POPE

DR. NOAH POPE HAS a thriving surgical practice. He cares deeply for his patients. He strives for excellence. Long ago, he realized perfection can never be achieved by humanity. However, he is also very aware that humans can come very close to perfection. That is what he calls advanced excellence. He was superior at achieving advanced excellence. He spent time in solitude each morning before beginning his day of complex heart surgeries, reminding himself and committing himself to advanced excellence.

Then he would go about accomplishing it. Every workday.

He asked the same of his staff. Advanced excellence were words used repeatedly throughout his surgical team.

Many lives have been restored by his advanced excellence efforts. He is committed to accomplishing results other surgeons only wish for but do not gain his success rate.

Due to Dr. Pope's stellar performance, he is honored for his performance and triumph in advanced heart surgeries. His techniques and expertise are studied and used as tools for training medical students.

Seldom has anyone ever had a success rate as his. He credited his success to his commitment to advanced excellence, his staff, and the desire of patients to be healed.

One gray overcast Georgia day, Dr. Pope had a surgery scheduled for a person with an aortic valve repair. Nothing really out of the ordinary. He had performed that surgery hundreds of times. He prepared as normal with time of meditation and solitude, striving for advanced excellence. Yet, he did not feel at peace as he entered the hospital and headed to the surgery center. He felt off. A feeling he had only felt a few times in his life. He didn't like it and had trouble shaking it off.

As he pulled on his scrubs, he reminded himself he was able and worthy to achieve advanced excellence. He had to admit to himself that he was still consumed with the delightful time he had on a date last night with Olivia.

He wondered if she could be the one he would ask to marry him. After all these years, he felt he had finally found the right woman. She was a true delight. She had her life in order. She no longer had to live out the learning phase of life. She had learned and now lived her belief system.

Olivia was also in her forties and had never been married. Just like Noah. It seemed like this was the ideal opportunity. No exes. No kids. No leftover baggage from abusive relationships. They both had joy in living life within their own realm. Having a spouse had never been a requirement for life achievement for either of them. They were both happy being single. For life? Why not?

They both knew the bow of single life was being bent toward the joy of matrimony.

They both lived highly moral lives. Ethics were a normalcy. Both Olivia and Noah wondered what making love with the other would be like. They were not advancing to sex until they were married. If that were to happen.

There was only one thing to resolve. Religion. Noah was a Universalist. Olivia was Christian. They were both quite unwilling to think of a change in their religion.

As Dr. Pope moved to the scrubbing station, he pondered her faith. He thought that Christianity was so simple. Too simple. Any ninny could be a Christian. It seemed all Christians had this dependency on Jesus. Couldn't they make it on their own? They all had brains and decision-making power. Why did they have to go to their God to find answers? Why did they have to pray to this Creator for guidance through anything? Or was it inability to get through everything? Whatever the answer, he didn't need it. He had brains and used them. He could make his own decisions. They weren't too big for him and his emotions. No, he could do without that Christian stuff. Not that he was snubbing his nose at it or condemning it. He just didn't need it. He was able on his own. Nothing had been too hard. He had been able to accomplish everything through his self-developed technique of advanced excellence. It had served him well and he will use it all his days.

The time had come for the surgery. He turned his attention to the surgery and doing his self-defined advanced excellence. He warmly greeted his medical team as he walked into the operating room. They responded with respect, admiration, and the same warmth.

The anesthesiologist gave Dr. Pope the information that the patient was ready. Dr. Pope began. As he worked, he listened to one of his favorite music pieces ever. He knew sometime he would have to check out this composer, Michael W. Smith. He loved this composition called "The Giving." It inspired him in such a profound way. Only Mozart's "Piano Concerto in C – Andante," had a greater effect on him. Both pieces took him to a place of elevated musical grandeur. They both lifted his soul to great joy.

As the procedure was underway, Dr. Pope slipped into reverie as he worked. Suddenly he realized something was wrong. This surgery was second nature; what happened? He had made a mistake. A failure. An unbelievable disaster. The patient was going to die. There was nothing he could do to save him, since he had severed the valve.

He had accomplished hundreds of aortic valve surgeries. How could this be? What had gone wrong? Dr. Pope knew it was his mistake. His fault. The man died. The rest of the team knew it was his fault. Slowly, they conclude the necessary processes.

Dr. Pope stumbles out of the operating room. He went through the motions of cleaning himself. He knows he must face the patient's family. He has done that many, many times. Usually he us bringing good news to the family. Occasionally, he had to bear the burden of conveying bad news. However, this is the first time it was his error and mistake that led to the demise of the patient.

What will he tell the patient's family? Will he tell them it was his mistake? If he does, they will sue him for more money than he will ever have. The hospital will be sued as well. Would it cost him his job? Maybe.

Others surgeons did not disclose their mistakes to the patient's family. They just said the surgery was not successful and the patient was unable to pull through due to his/her condition. They got by without explaining their mistakes. Everyone makes mistakes. Dr. Pope realized he was one of those people too. Still, he was not one of the other surgeons. He was Dr. Pope. He couldn't just say death was due to the patient's condition. Or could he?

He could not decide what to do. But he must.

He realized the staff was fully aware of his mistake. What if they revealed his mistake? What would the effect be on his reputation and his advanced excellence lifestyle? He can't let his reputation be damaged, can he? Or can he provide detailed information to all those who follow his strategic lifestyle, by indicating that on that particular day that was his advanced excellence?

That didn't make any sense and he knew it.

He knew it was his mistake. Would he cover it up? Let it blow over? Hope his medical team doesn't reveal the truth? Or will he tell the truth to all and everyone? He wants to do the latter but does he have the courage to face all that comes with it.

What to do? He is confused, conflicted, and grieving the loss of the patient. There is no time to delay. He has to go speak to the patient's family. Yet, what will he tell them? Dr. Pope was confused and confounded. He did not know what to do. He had to communicate with the patient's family in just a few minutes.

The decision would not come to Noah. At last, he has an epiphany. He will call Olivia, explain the truth to her. She is a Christian. She could ask her God what he should do. Maybe there is something to this simplicity of Christian religion and everyone needing God at some point.

If You Were God

You have watched Noah's entire life. You have seen his successes and his life of grandeur. Time and time again you have sent messages through your Instructors to get him to turn to you. To worship you and love you.

He could achieve so much more if he would allow your influence in his life. What is wrong with him? Doesn't he want even better than he has it now?

Noah didn't listen. He went his own way, utilizing the great gifts I have provided him at his creation. He used them in a way to promote himself and to create his own form of religion, advanced excellence. I didn't send that to him but I do like it. It makes sense to do your very best every day. However, everyone will have a time when achieving in your own strength won't fulfill everything.

Just as you knew, a mistake was coming. He didn't listen to your Instructors' pleas, but went ahead on his own.

Now look what happened. Should I take him back now that he is in trouble and needs me to help him through? Or should I just let him go on his own as he has before and watch his life, relationships, and career be destroyed?

I gave him tons of chances and opportunities galore. His conclusion was to go his own way and do life his way.

What shall I do? He is a cool guy and committed to morals and ethics. But that is not a commitment to serving and loving me.

I will think about it and get back with him soon. I have a lot of other impossible situations to resolve. Like millions of other things.

What God Will Do

My son, Noah, come to me. I will give you rest, comfort, and love. Jesus said while He was on earth that all who are heavy laden should come to Him and He will give them rest.

God is a God of love. Not a God of condemnation, if we will come to Him, ask Jesus to be our Savior and openly confess that He is Lord of our life.

God encourages Noah to tell the truth. That he will see Noah through this valley of great difficulty (Psalm 23:4). His love will be poured out onto Noah and His hand of guidance will be upon him.

While Noah will need to face the consequences of his mistake, God will remind him of all the beautiful, wonderful, successful surgeries he has accomplished. No one can take away those good consequences from him either.

Once Noah asks Jesus to be a Savior, he will find the comfort of Jesus' love and have peace beyond any peace this world can provide (John 14:27, John 16:33, 2 Peter 1:2).

Olivia will be by Noah's side when he lives out the truth of his mistake. Her hand of comfort will be upon his shoulder. She is a conduit between God and

Noah. God's love will permeate through her onto Noah (John 13:34-35, 1 John 2:7).

Because of God's divine guidance, Noah will be able to find joy in life (Psalm 16:11) as he goes through whatever his admission of mistake will bring (2 Corinthians 7:10). He will have sorrow, regret and grief over his mistake, but God's counsel will be words of forgiveness and new beginnings (Lam. 3:23).

Life will still bring contentment and joy to Noah because he now lives for God. Giving his best to the Lord is his desire.

John 14:27 I am leaving you with a gift—peace of mind and heart. And the peace I give is a gift the world cannot give. So don't be troubled or afraid.

John 16:33 I have told you all this so that you may have peace in me. Here on earth, you will have many trials and sorrows. But take heart, because I have overcome the world.

2 Peter 1:2 May God give you more and more grace and peace as you grow in your knowledge of God and Jesus our Lord.

John 13:34-35 So now I am giving you a new commandment: Love each other. Just as I have loved you, you should love each other. 35 Your love for one another will prove to the world that you are my disciples.

1. **John 2:7** Dear friends, I am not writing a new commandment for you; rather it is an old one you have had from the very beginning. This old commandment—to love one another—is the same message you heard before.

Psalm 16:11 You will show me the way of life, granting me the joy of your presence and the pleasures of living with you forever.

1. **Corinthians 7:10** For the kind of sorrow God wants us to experience leads us away from sin and results in salvation. There's no regret for that kind of sorrow. But worldly sorrow, which lacks repentance, results in spiritual death.

Lamentations 3:23 Great is his faithfulness; his mercies begin afresh each morning.

Chapter Ten

TAKING BACK LOST GROUND

LIFE WAS OKAY WHEN Ian was young. Or so he thought. Of course it was the only life he knew. His life experiences were his and he did not really know how other lives were lived except for the few details he heard from other school kids.

Ian did not oppose his life and the family environment. It was just what it was. Recently he noticed a change in his parents. Neither one was happy. They were arguing a lot more than they used to argue. There didn't seem to be any unity any longer. It appeared as if something was going to break.

Often he thought and pondered about what was going on with his parents as they were not happy with him either. It seemed that nearly every day one or both of them were angry with him. He tried to do better. He tried to do his best. But really all these problems at home were getting to him.

He thought about the happiness in his family continuously. He had difficulty sleeping at night. After his parents told him to go to bed, which meant they no longer tucked him in bed or prayed a good night prayer or told him that they loved him. Now it was just time for bed, good night, and sleep well. He could hear them arguing almost every night after he was in bed. It was awful. He couldn't stand it. He couldn't sleep with all the fighting and destructive words he heard.

Before the fighting ended, he heard accusing things like his mom continually saying "How could you?" She said, "Don't I mean anything to you?" She said, "I am your wife. How am I supposed to accept this?"

His dad replied that it happened because she treated him so badly. That she should have continued to have sex with him after Ian was born. "How could she stop, his dad asked her." He said, "What is wrong with me that you don't want me anymore?" He said, "Did you just expect me to never have sex again in my life?"

And on and on and on it went. Repeated so often. The same things over and over. Never any resolve. No solution. Just arguing. More and more arguing, with raised voices and many accusations.

Ian wondered what had happened. What had caused all the disruption? Someone must have caused it. He was only seven and it was hard to understand. He wanted to know. His emotions were frayed. He didn't know what he could do or not do at home anymore because seemingly everything he did would land him in big-time trouble. Then he was disciplined and life would get even more upset. His anxiety was off the charts. He was overwhelmingly stressed. The situation at home was all he thought about. It was on his mind constantly.

Ian's grades slipped. He was unable to participate in school. He couldn't concentrate on what the teacher was teaching. He could only focus on his family problems. He wanted them fixed and life returned to normal. No more of this arguing and yelling and him being in trouble all the time. But no matter what he thought or tried at home, nothing worked to make things better.

His friends even asked him if he was okay. They saw a different Ian. He became a recluse. His friends started playing without him at recess and at lunchtime, and some days he ate alone. He was being consumed by the problems at home.

Ian had no happiness or fun. He was in trouble at school for not learning and participating. At home, he was always doing something wrong and getting in trouble. He couldn't eat because of the family disruption. Ian couldn't sleep at night because his parents were fighting again and again.

Even when they went to their separate rooms and went to sleep, he would lay wide eyed staring into the abyss.

Ian wished he could die. He could not go on like this much longer. Things only got worse, not better. A change came, his parents were no longer arguing.T hey were not talking to each other and trying their best to ignore each other. They both started talking and interacting more with Ian. Initially that was fun for Ian.

But he soon noticed that if he was having fun with his mom, his dad would be upset. And vice versa. Ian loved them both and did not know what to do.

Eventually, this new family life added even more stress to this already devastated young boy. He knew he was about to break. Something was going to happen inside him if things didn't somehow get better. He decided he wanted to die. Yet, had no idea how he could.

Ian wondered over and over, who is to blame? Somebody had to be to blame for his family falling apart. Who was it? Was it his dad or his mom? Or was it him? Ian thought hard about it and came to a seven-year-old's conclusion that it had to be him!

No one else could have caused it. As he looked back, he could remember getting in trouble one night. That was the night the arguing started. That was it. He finally figured it out. It had to be him. Because he got in trouble that night, everything fell apart. Now look at all the damage. His parents were so angry at each other that they wouldn't even talk.

What could he do to fix it?

That night while he was in bed listening, he heard his parents return to the days of old. Arguing, fighting, bickering, badgering, and now even yelling. No one could sleep through that.

Something was going down. He just knew it. Suddenly he heard his dad stomp to the bedroom. He came out a few minutes later and blurted out to his wife that she should tell Ian he loves him and would be back to see him.

His mom said she wouldn't say it for him. That if he really loved him, he would tell him himself. Ian's dad came rushing into his bedroom. He saw Ian was awake and said hurriedly that he loved him. He also said that he had to leave now and be gone for a time but he would be back to see Ian.

With that, his dad left with a violent slamming of the front door. Ian could hear his mom crying in the living room. He didn't know what to do. He was too paralyzed emotionally to know what to do. So, he just stayed there in bed doing the same nothing he had done for the last six months.

The next morning, his mom looked like she had not slept as she explained to Ian what had happened. She didn't tell Ian bad things about his dad, but she did say they were getting a divorce.

Ian, in the midst of all this emotional crises, released his pain and agony and wept bitterly. He didn't want his family broken up. He wanted things fixed and a return to a life of happiness like they used to have. But now, it would not work out the way he wanted it to happen. Somebody had to be at fault. Someone caused this divorce. Ian knew that it was him. He wept and mourned like never before in his life. He wanted to die.

The divorce happened within a short few months. His dad came to see him a few times but it was not the same. His mom tried to show Ian he was loved as she observed how much the divorce had damaged him. Ian didn't buy into this new display of love. He knew the divorce was his fault.

From the time of his decision, his life was marred. He continued blaming himself for his parents' divorce, which influenced all facets of his life. He did not have many friends or deep relationships. Ian had a lack of interest for almost everything, including school and his grades.

In his teens, he did find solace in detailing cars. He was good at it. He was proud of how he could make a car or truck glisten and shine. He felt comfort in doing it and a sense of worth as he detailed the cars. He told himself that he was kind of like the Karate Kid, "wax on, and wax off, " when Mr. Miyagi taught the Karate Kid how to wax cars properly.

He was proud of his work. Friends started having him detail their vehicles. It slowly turned into a side hustle. Everyone was pleased with his work. But his dad never saw his work, as they remained estranged.

During his junior year in high school, something clicked one day that he would need to go to college to get a degree so he could make something of himself someday. From that day forward, Ian was on target to improve his GPA so he could go to college. He took the SAT and scored well. He surprised himself.

Maybe, just maybe, he could improve his grades enough to get accepted to a college of worth and obtain financial aid. Neither his mom nor dad had saved any money for him to go to college. His mom could barely scrape by and his dad, well, he didn't know if he had money or not. Ian was certainly not going to ask him for any.

Ian accomplished his goal and managed to build his GPA to 3.24 by the time he graduated.

While other kids were celebrating and whooping it up on graduation day, Ian was somber and took part in graduation without fan fare. Ian pretended that he was not interested. He was still pondering and living how he was the reason for his parents' divorce.

He was accepted at a Colorado state college. He received financial aid and was also able to do a little work detailing cars, even though there were not many cars on campus.

During college, he opted out of biology by taking an astronomy class. He was intrigued with astronomy. He settled on astronomy as his major, after discovering that he could find work carrying o u t astronomy research projects. He enjoyed pursuing his career and readied himself for his future working in that profession. He hoped and dreamed of having a corner work cubicle where he could dive into his work and not have to be a bubbly and outgoing worker.

Ian settled in on astronomy as his life career. He studied feverishly on all astronomy-related classes. As he was looking for a research career, he seriously applied himself to writing courses.

He made the dean's list and was happy but not joyful. Not overjoyed. He had the overhanging guilt of causing his parents' divorce. Or so he had convinced himself. Graduation day arrived but he saw no reason to walk during commencement. Instead, he packed up his possessions, including the list of astronomy research companies, and went to his mom's house.

At his mom's house, their relationship remained unchanged. She congratulated him for graduating, then asked, but why astronomy? Can you even get a job as an astronomer? Ian withdrew to his room.

That statement motivated Ian to land a job in the career he selected. The following morning, he completed his resume and filed it with the research companies he had identified were a fit for him. He hit the submit button with the companies and waited.

It seemed like a very long wait, however, it was only three days. There was interest at one company in Southern California. The following day he had a telephone interview. That seemed to go well. A day after that he had a live interview over social media. Ian thought that one went well. He found out the following day the company thought so too. They invited him to San Diego for an interview. He was excited to be able to have a hands on tour of the Mount Laguna Observatory, commonly known in his profession as MLO.

The tour and interview went well. He did not have to fake it and act like someone he was not. He was just himself. At the conclusion of the interview and tour, he was offered a research position, working at the observatory. He would be employed by San Diego State University, which owns and operates the observatory.

Ian was finally excited about something. He had landed a job. Now for the rest of getting to work. He needed to find an apartment and get a car.

When they made the salary offer, he knew it would be a battle to afford living in the area. He had looked at housing just in case he landed the job. He also checked with an auto dealership, and he would qualify as a first-time buyer once he was hired.

The salary was less than he hoped for but he found a little place in Ramona. A studio apartment. Ian was thankful it was furnished. He signed a month-to-month lease. Then he went to the local Ford dealership and purchased a car. Between the rent and car payment he would have very little left over. That was okay with Ian because he wasn't planning a social life anyway.

He moved and settled into the studio apartment. His first days at work went well. He was happy about what he was doing. He didn't get the corner but he had a cubicle. He made it his. He worked diligently. Many days working late.

He met another newbie. William seemed like a good guy. He didn't ask Ian too many questions and was committed to his work.

They starting hanging out at lunch and formed a friendship.

Over time they discovered they both had the same situation. They loved the job but could hardly survive financially. One day William proposed that they move in together in a two-bedroom apartment as they would both have a little more leftover money at the end of the month. Ian pondered the idea. He wasn't very keen on it but he did have a goal to pay off his car way earlier than required. After a week or so, he agreed.

They found a spot and moved to El Cajon. Not a top-shelf community but it was fine for both of them.

Ian soon found out that William had it together. He enjoyed life and all its attributes. It seemed he did not have anything dragging him down. He was upbeat and showed genuine friendship to Ian.

Ian wanted to give in and have William as a real true friend. A comrade, so to speak. However, he kept asking himself if he would ruin William's life too. Just like he had instigated his parents' divorce.

Over time, William's vivacious ways led to Ian opening up and living as the real person he was. Yet there was always something holding him back from letting him completely enjoy the friendship.

William was savvy enough to recognize Ian was holding back. That something was depressing him. That something affected his life so that he couldn't enjoy it. He asked Ian about it. Ian wasn't ready to talk about it and let William know that as kindly as he could.

As the year advanced, William and Ian became close friends. Slowly, over a series of deep talks, Ian relayed to William about his parents' divorce and how it was his fault. William, being a friend of conviction would not, could not accept that Ian was the cause of the divorce. As they reviewed the divorce process of Ian's parents, William discerned that Ian's dad had an affair and that his dad and mom could never get past that. That led to their divorce. It wasn't Ian's fault.

Ian was amazed he had never thought of that. He just knew it was his fault. It was not easy for Ian to change his thinking or life. He had lived fifteen years within the shell of self-condemnation. He slowly came to the realization that he had missed out on fifteen years of life due to his selfabasement. While the discovery was a good thing, he was unable to switch gears. He was consumed with depression and self-condemnation. Ian had a hard time figuring out how to live life differently. William tried to help him with it, but Ian just couldn't seem to get going with his newly discovered liberty.

Ian knew the truth now and wanted to change and enjoy all aspects of life. How could he do that? He didn't know. William came up with an idea. He encouraged Ian to go to counseling. Ian initially thought that was stupid. Only sick people go to a shrink. Besides the few co-workers would make fun of him because he couldn't make it on his own.

After a few months, Ian finally gave in to William's persistence. He would go to counseling. But just once to check it out. William was ecstatic. He even found a counseling service at a local church that had free counseling to help people from the community. Ian said he was not sure about going to a counselor at a church. He hadn't gone to a church in years. His mom stopped taking him to church after the divorce. Ian looked for other counseling services but they were way expensive. Ian procrastinated. That did not help him at all. He knew it too.

William was insistent and pestered Ian about going. Finally, Ian gave in to going to one session. William was thrilled and called to make the appointment for him. The admin said that the counselor (Mr. Welling) would like to meet Ian after church service the following Sunday so he could tell Ian what the counseling would be like.

Ian was not keen on the idea of going to church. William knew that he would not be, so he suggested he would go with him. So off they went. The service had some moments of interest. Ian liked the band. The lead guitarist could lay down the riffs.

After the service, he met Mr. Welling in his office, as instructed. Mr. Welling was a calm, kind man with a genuine spirit. After a conversation about what to expect in the sessionsIan stopped him right there and said he was only promising to come to one session. Mr. Welling said he was willing to have that one meeting.

The following Tuesday afternoon Ian went to the session. As he walked to Mr. Welling's office, he thought of William's words of encouragement. Ian felt deep gratitude that he had found a co-worker and roommate who cared about him, far more than Ian thought possible. William was such a remarkable friend.

Mr. Welling, again, was kind and gentle. Ian was quite surprised as he had not had a male figure in his life who portrayed that. Mr. Welling asked about Ian's life and of course his parents' divorce just came tumbling out of Ian's mouth. He concluded the story by explaining to Mr. Welling that the divorce was his fault.

As he was talking, Mr. Welling listened intently and took some notes. While telling the story, Ian could see that Mr. Welling was disturbed when he told him that he was the reason for the divorce. He wasn't looking at Mr. Welling while he told the story. He looked at the floor and out the window while he spoke. Yet he knew Mr. Welling cared. That drew him in.

After fifty minutes, Ian had relayed the story of most of the divorce and his role in it. He spoke of life without his dad and living with his mom who was fractured emotionally. Mr. Welling said that it was time to conclude for the day. Ian wondered when he was going to offer him some counsel. Why hadn't he jumped in to say something when Ian was telling his life story?

Then he asked Ian the question Ian did not want to hear. Would he come back so that Mr. Welling could share a few things with him? Ian, somewhat begrudgingly, agreed. He was kind of resistant but also a little intrigued to see what Mr. Welling thought of the whole situation.

As they closed the session, Mr. Welling asked if he could share something from the Bible. Ian said it was okay. Mr. Welling turned to a place in the Bible where it said, "For God so loved the world that he gave His only son to, so that everyone who believes in Him will not perish, but have eternal life" (John 3:16). Mr. Welling also read other words from the Bible, "The LORD is good, a stronghold in the day of trouble, and He knows those who take refuge in Him" (Nahum 1:7). He read more words to Ian, "Behold I am with you and will keep you wherever you go" (Genesis 28:15). Mr. Welling read one last verse, "But as many as received Him, to them He gave the right to become children of God, to those who believe in His name" (John 1:12).

As a going away instruction, he asked Ian to look those verses up in the Bible and read them each day. Mr. Welling showed him a Bible app on his phone he could download.

Ian could not identify what it was but he felt a bit better about himself. He didn't know why but it was a good feeling. He hadn't had good feelings about himself for a long, long time.

William was enthused about what Ian told him. He told Ian that maybe they should go to that church again next Sunday. Ian felt confused and perplexed about church.

They went to church the next Sunday. The sermon was about some guy named Joshua who was going to be the new leader of a group of people called Israelites. They were supposed to take over a country. Joshua, the new leader, was told by God to take the country. God gave him a plan and told Joshua to complete it. Joshua was fearful,

unsure of himself, questioning if he could really lead those people. God saw Joshua's humanness and gave him direct instruction of how to lead the people.

Lead like the man who was the previous leader, Moses. You were his assistant. God said, so step up remember how Moses led, follow my commandments and the words of my direction. God said if you do, you will be victorious and the land will be yours. His instructions to Joshua were to be strong and courageous. Do not be terrified or dismayed. Then God said to Joshua that He would be with him wherever he goes. Joshua declared he would do so. He went on to lead the Israelites to a tremendous victory.

Ian was taken by that story. An assistant to the leader was given a huge opportunity. Not only given the responsibility but given instructions from God. Instructions that he should follow God totally, listen for his instructions, be strong and courageous, and to not be terrified because God would be with him in all things. In all ways.

That really resonated with Ian. He wondered if God would strengthen him, make him courageous, and help him give up his inability to beat depression. As Ian stopped day dreaming and began listening to the sermon again, he heard the pastor say that everyone can receive these same gifts from God. That God loved everyone, all people everywhere, that He sent His only Son to come to earth and pay the price of the sin of everyone so that every person could join God's family and have eternal life with Him. The pastor described how the Son (Jesus Christ) came down from heaven to earth. He took on the appearance of a man even though he was God. One of the triune God. The others were Lord God Our Father and the Holy Spirit. Jesus came with one purpose, to suffer and die so that all humans' sins could be forgiven and they could have a glorious eternity with God in heaven.

Something came over Ian as he heard that. A warmth, a glow, and a kind of feeling he never had before. It included a calling, a plea, to come. Come to Jesus and be saved. Receive his love and be a part of God's family. Both now and forever.

The pastor asked if anyone wanted to publicly receive Jesus as their Savior. He said it was a free gift. Anyone who confessed Jesus as Savior would receive Jesus into their lives as their Savior.

For some reason Ian could not hold back. He stepped out of the pew and went to the altar where there were others who did the same. They were prayed over and they prayed with the pastor in receiving Jesus as their Savior. The group of new believers were escorted to another room where they were provided information of how to begin reading the Bible and praying. They were invited back to church and also invited to a small group where they could learn more.

Ian left gratified. William had waited around and greeted him with a huge smile. Ian began talking about how wonderful it was but wondered if he could break down the door of depression.

That week he met with Mr. Welling who listened with joy of Ian's newfound faith. Ian talked about wanting Joshua's strength and courage, and to be able to overcome his depression. Mr. Welling asked if Ian would like to pray about it and then they would do an exercise. Ian tried to pray but it seemed all jumbled up words. Mr. Welling was not adversely affected by a lack of a great sounding prayer.

He led Ian to an exercise where Ian could identify things that brought him happiness and contentment. Also, he identified things that brought his depression on.

Ian and Mr. Welling continued to meet on a weekly basis. Over time, Ian could see he was changing. He started feeling better about himself and lived a life of greater happiness.

Mr. Welling helped him to understand his inner self by having Ian complete a Self-Compass Inventory. The result of the inventory exercise was that Ian was a withdrawn person. Being weak as a trend, rather than asserting; lacking strength and missing out on love. He and Mr. Welling began working toward him gaining confidence and being able to express his love for others and having the courage (strength) to do it.

One day, Mr. Welling told him of the difference between joy and happiness. That joy comes when we surrender ourselves to God and live for and with Him. Once we trust fully in the Lord and give up on just our own understanding, we can find peace and joy abundantly. Mr. Welling referenced, Isaiah 26:3, Proverbs 3:5-6, Psalm 37:3-5, and Psalm 16:11.

Ian left the counseling session that day committed to establishing that form of life for himself. The process went pretty well, but there was still something else. Something he had not yet recognized.

At his next counseling session, Mr. Welling introduced him to the concept that enabled Ian to soar to total release and liberty. Ian read the verse from

2 Corinthians 5:17. "Therefore, if anyone is in Christ, the creation has come. The old has gone, the new is here!" That did it for Ian. It propelled him from being stuck in his old self-condemnation to being a new creature. Forgiven, alive, liberated, and loved. He was a new man from that moment on.

Not that there weren't moments when his old self wanted to take control, but Ian was most proficient at allowing his brain to dominate his negative emotions. He came to believe and live fully without reserve.

As a workday is drawing to a close some ten years later, Ian closes his laptop and reflects on the last season of time. He contemplates how life is different now and has been for a decade.

Wow, those who knew him in high school would not know him now.

Maybe he should attend the next class reunion.

He ponders how good life has become. Dedicated to God and showing his love for Him and for others. It has made all the difference. Ian is doing very well at work and has been promoted. He is very involved in his church. He even leads a small group. He has joined a single's group from church. There is a woman in the group that has caught Ian's eye. Ian now knows how life was meant to be.

If You Were God

Hey, look at Ian. He finally got everything I was sending his way. It certainly took him long enough. But now he has got it. I was about to give up on him. He is truly committed to me. Just like the instructions I give all people.

Commit your life to me and I will be your God. If not, I will just let you go your own way and you can experience a dreaded, nonfunctioning, hopeless life. That is what is going on with Ian's mother. If she would just turn to me, I could give her counsel and life could improve. Life could become good again. There could even be another man for her. But she is stuck and won't turn to me. So suffering is what she will do now. If she ever wises up, she can have a completely fulfilling life.

Then there is Ian's dad. What's up with him? Stuck on himself. Made irreparable mistakes in his marriage. Saw that his son was drastically affected by the divorce and just walked away. While I am not saying I will never forgive him if he turns and comes to me, but right now he is on a direct path to hell. I am not sending anyone to directly influence him anymore. I gave way too much of myself to win him over to becoming a child of my family. But no, he wanted only his own selfish way. Now he has it and he is miserable. Everything he has touched has failed. Because he only thinks of himself. Not once has he even turned to me. Yes, he is bound for hell unless he completely changes.

What God Will Do

Ian, my son, you are adopted into my family. Into my kingdom. Into eternal life with me. Your eternal life with me began that day you accepted my Son Jesus as your Savior. That day you acted after you heard that message about Joshua.

I am so thankful that you listened to Mr. Welling who loves me and serves me with a heart for others. He prayed over you for a long time. He prayed how he could best prepare to meet with you and how to counsel you. Mr. Welling heard from my Holy Spirit to share with you 2 Corinthians 5:17. It is the verse that changed your life.

Now you are liberated from your captivity (Isaiah 61:1-4) and you can recognize my never-ending love for you. Even when you make mistakes or sin, I am here for you. When you confess your sin, I will lift you up, dust you off, and set you back on the path of right living (Psalm 103:11-13).

Ian, your love toward me makes me abound in joy. I was there by your side when I created you with special gifts and abilities (Psalm 139:13-18). Now you are using them and for the best purpose. To influence others to come to faith in me, carrying out my mission of spreading the good news to everyone you encounter (Acts 1:8, Matt.28:19-20).

As you now know, living in the depraved world where sin abounds, there will be valleys, hurdles, and difficulties. But through your faith in me and abiding with Jesus, your Savior, your trust in me remains (John 15:5-8). How beautiful it is to declare that you are a child of mine forever (John 1:12)!

2 Corinthians 5:17 This means that anyone who belongs to Christ has become a new person. The old life is gone; a new life has begun!

Isaiah 61:1-4 The Spirit of the Sovereign Lord is upon me, for the Lord has anointed me to bring good news to the poor. He has sent me to comfort the brokenhearted and to proclaim that captives will be released and prisoners will be freed. 2 He has sent me to tell those who mourn that the time of the Lord's favor has come, and with it, the day of God's anger against their enemies. 3 To all who mourn in Israel, he will give a crown of beauty for ashes, a joyous blessing instead of mourning, festive praise instead of despair. In their righteousness, they will be like great oaks that the Lord has planted for his own glory. 4 They will rebuild the ancient ruins, repairing cities destroyed long ago. They will revive them, though they have been deserted for many generations.

Psalm 103:11-13 For his unfailing love toward those who fear him is as great as the height of the heavens above the earth. 12 He has removed our sins as far from us as the east is from the west. 13 The Lord is like a father to his children, tender and compassionate to those who fear him.

Psalm 139:13-18 You made all the delicate, inner parts of my body and knit me together in my mother's womb. 14 Thank you for making me so wonderfully complex! Your workmanship is marvelous— how well I know it. 15 You watched me as I was being formed in utter seclusion, as I was woven together in the dark of the womb. 16 You saw me before I was born. Every day of my life was recorded in your book. Every moment was laid out before a single day had passed. 17 How precious are your thoughts about me, O God. They cannot be numbered! 18 I can't even count them; they outnumber the grains of sand! And when I wake up, you are still with me!

Acts 1:8 But you will receive power when the Holy Spirit comes upon you. And you will be my witnesses, telling people about me everywhere—in Jerusalem, throughout Judea, in Samaria, and to the ends of the earth.

Matthew 28:19-20 Therefore, go and make disciples of all the nations, baptizing them in the name of the Father and the Son and the Holy Spirit. 20 Teach these new disciples to obey all the commands I have given you. And be sure of this: I am with you always, even to the end of the age.

John 15:5-8 Yes, I am the vine; you are the branches. Those who remain in me, and I in them, will produce much fruit. For apart from me you can do nothing. 6 Anyone who does not remain in me is thrown away like a useless branch and withers. Such branches are gathered into a pile to be burned. 7 But if you remain in me and my words remain in you, you may ask for anything you want, and it will be granted! 8 When you produce much fruit, you are my true disciples. This brings great glory to my Father.

John 1:12 But to all who believed him and accepted him, he gave the right to become children of God.

Chapter Eleven

THE ATHLETE

JOSH WAS AN ABOVE-AVERAGE athlete. He excelled in sports as a youth. He could run like the wind. He thought running was the coolest thing. He loved the runner's high! In high school his results were stunning. He was undefeated in the 400 meters. Yes, he won the state title. Pretty good for a state known for runners... Arkansas. University of Arkansas provided him a scholarship to attend their school and to join the track and field team. Who would turn that down? Well, Josh did. He had his sights on the West Coast. Eventually he signed with the University of Oregon. The prestigious West Coast school known for developing world-renowned track and field athletes. There was Hayward Field and the elite Prefontaine Classic Track & Field meet. Josh could not pass that up. Plus, he could live in another part of the country.

Josh soon found out there was stiff competition at U of O, the Pac 12, and throughout the country. He really had to train and give exemplary effort. He was willing. Josh knew it was his big chance in life. Only four years to prove himself and then turn pro. He dreamed that someday he would be a Diamond League champion, win a World Championship, and a gold medal at the Olympics. Then he would get sponsors, do commercials, and be a celebrity track star in America. But he had a lot to accomplish before then.

Josh had good success, due to his commitment to become the best 400-meter runner in the world. He excelled as a freshman, winning the conference 400-meter run. That was quite amazing. Winning the conference championship in his freshman year.

No way was Josh letting that go to his head. He had much, much more to accomplish. He dreamed of winning the World Championship and the Olympic gold medal. Josh was no longer settling for the Diamond League Championship.

Over the next three years, Josh only had a few stumbles on his way to his goal. But he considered them as learning lessons. He trained even harder. He excelled in both training and competitions. He was moving toward his goal of becoming the best 400-meter runner in the world. He had now added an initial facet to his goal; he set a goal of setting the world's record in 400 meters. He remembers how Michael Johnson set the 400-meter world record in 1999. It was time for an American to hold the world record again. Josh is truly convinced he can do the same. These two goals are his greatest aspirations in life. Nothing else really matters.

Josh has little time for anything else. A girl he liked in high school and dated a few times is still in the forefront of his memory, but there is no time for that now. His parents and siblings have come to understand that Josh really is not a part of their lives any longer. He has moved on and seldom calls or texts. He does not send birthday greetings or show much of any feeling of fondness. He did go to the family Christmas last year but spent most of the day training. He barely had time for anyone. Not even time for his little brother, Lucas, who idolized him and Josh knew it. He had dinner with the family but didn't eat hardly any of the food they prepared as it was not on his training diet. His mother was so disappointed. She had spent hours preparing Josh's favorite dishes.

It was the next spring season that Josh came to realize that his talent was good, very good, but not the best in the world. He won nearly every race he entered, but there were a couple of other runners who excelled. Their times were better than Josh's. No matter how much he trained, he could not reach their times.

He became dismayed. He had to be the best in the world.

One day he decided to go to a local downtown gym for a change of pace and hoped to gain a different perspective. As he began his workout, he felt like something good was about to happen. Suddenly, another young man appeared before him. It was Levi, a fellow track team member from his high school. Levi was a couple years older and participated in field events. He was a good long jumper. Josh lost contact with him after Levi graduated.

Levi had gone to college without a track scholarship. He was like 95% of athletes, who took up a career other than sports, after college. He had studied business management in college. He became a sports coach and trainer at a franchise gym. Levi worked hard and was committed to advancing in the company as his starting pay grade didn't cut it for his lifestyle.

Over a two two year period, he moved his way up and became a manager of a franchise in Eugene, OR.

Such a coincidence that Josh ran into him at the gym. They chatted for a minute and Levi asked him to stop by his office before he left. Josh was happy to do so.

Levi wanted to join Josh for a healthy meal but needed to finish a couple of things. Josh waited around while he finished things.

Over dinner, they talked about Josh's career. Levi had continued to follow it. As they caught up with where Josh was in his career now, he expressed his frustration that he could not gain time and keep up with the best in the world. He said that there must be something he could do to himself to get that extra 1.5 seconds he needed.

After hearing that, Levi leaned forward, lowered his voice, and said there was. Josh leaned in and listened closely. Levi told him of these steroids he had access to that did just enough to get athletes to an improved performance level. He said they worked for everyone.

Plus, they were nearly impossible to detect in urine tests.

Josh thought of the disgust he had for HGH athletes who had to resort to chemicals to get to a higher level. Plus, he remembered how they were stripped of awards and medals, banished by the Olympic committee and other governing bodies, and persecuted by the fans. Not to mention they lost their commercial financial sponsors.

His head was spinning. He couldn't do that. He would get caught. He wouldn't be able to live with himself. Even if he set a world's record, he would never be able to fully accept the notoriety because he cheated. He quickly made up his mind and told Levi he wasn't interested.

Levi didn't press him. They finished dining and were parting ways when Levi told Josh that he now had his contact info and if he ever needed anything to give him a call.

Over the next season, Josh excelled in college track. His was winning all races. But he was still about two seconds behind the times of the best in the world. Those pro athletes were doing better and he couldn't keep up.

Josh was gearing up for the NCAA outdoor 400.

He thought of how hard he was trying. He was excelling beyond everyone's expectations. Except for his coach and himself. There had to be a way to do better. But what? He was at his wits' end. As he pondered all possibilities for improved training, diet, workouts, etc., he suddenly thought of Levi.

Josh immediately wished he had not thought of the option Levi made available. Over the next weeks, nothing improved. The only thing that happened was that he was becoming consumed with the thought of Levi's option.

One evening. after an exhausting day of training and no sign of improvement, he gave in and called Levi.

Levi asked if he was sure. Josh said he wasn't but needed to try something. So they met. Levi said he would take care of the cost for a month. Josh didn't even want to know the cost. He knew he wouldn't be able to afford. So he decided upon a month. That was it.

He started taking the steroids. Secretly, of course. No one knew and he wasn't telling anyone. He couldn't risk getting caught. There was virtually no change in his times for over a week. But then something started to change. His times picked up. His times increased by about a second.

Then the season came to an end after he won the NCAA 400 - meter outdoor race. He set a new collegiate record.

He wasn't satisfied. He needed to be faster. He reached out to evi. They struck a deal. Levi would provide him the steroids for a 10% payment of the sponsorships he gets after he turned pro. A deal for two years. Josh agreed so he could have the steroids.

His time had qualified him for the Millrose games early the next year. Millrose games were considered the most prestigious indoor track and field competition. He trained exceptionally hard for that competition.

The big day came on a cold and cloudy New York City winter's day. Josh was ready. He could hardly sleep.

The big race was challenging and took the best of Josh's effort. But he prevailed and won the event. His time was good, really good. Well, not a Millrose games record or a best in the world time this year, but it was superior. It would lead to being invited to many competitions that year.

After his victory interviews, he was invited by an official to the official room for his urine test. Josh hadn't taken those before and was nervous because of his steroid use. But he kept telling himself that Levi promised himself that it was virtually undetectable.

He finished and headed back to the hotel. His coach wanted to take him out for a celebration meal. As he was getting ready, there was a loud knock on the door. He looked at his watch and realized it wasn't time for the coach to be there yet.

He wondered who it was.

He slowly went to the door and peered through the peep hole. It was his coach. So he gladly opened the door. He was excited to celebrate with his coach.

His coach flew into the room, slammed the door shut, and vomited out the words, "You failed the drug test."

Josh sunk onto the bed, knowing his life had changed forever. Nothing would ever be right again. He would be banned from running.

Josh mumbled, "God help me."

If You Were God

I adorned Josh with so much talent. He had great ability. He should have looked to me for guidance and counsel before turning to steroids that would eventually catch up with him. Of course, they do. He thought of himself as a numb skull. Everybody knows you can't get away with that. I am not protecting anyone from the law. Anyone who goes against me and tries to find answers on their own will pay for it. . Now he can pay the price. Josh should have looked to me before the fact, not waiting until after the deeds were done. So his career is finished. He can get a job. Maybe he will find a woman someday who will be compassionate and be his bride. But he can't expect me to do anything for him. The door is closed. He didn't come to me so he can live with his decisions and the accompanying consequences.

What God Would Do

Josh, my son, come to me. Turn to me and draw close. I will draw near to you (James 4:7-8). I am still your God. Your Savior (Jonah 2:9). The one who is able to forgive you as far as the east is from the west (Psalm 103:12). I will remember your sins no more once you have confessed your sin to me and sought forgiveness (Isaiah 43:25). No price to pay. The price of your sins has already been paid by my Son, your Savior, Jesus Christ (Isaiah 53:4-11).

Though you will have earthly consequences due to your illegal activities and resulting expulsion from the track and field world, I will now be by your side seeing you through all things as long as you are seeking me to help you through (Colossians 1: 21-23).

While it was wrong of you to look away from me as you became a star in the track and field world, I come with open arms to welcome you to me and my kingdom. You see, I am a jealous God seeking all to live and serve me all the days of their lives. Yet I am also a forgiving God and will not stay angry. I will forgive and restore our relationship and provide eternal life for those who come to me with sincere hearts (Colossians 1:13-14, Ephesians 1:7-14).

Josh, as you go through this dark valley of life, I will be with you (Psalm 23:4), I will not leave you or forsake you (Hebrews 13:5b, Joshua 1:5). I am urging you to become a spokesman for me and for promoting a clean sport of no illegal performanceenhancing drugs.

Seek me every day and I will be yours...forever (1 John 4: 9)!

James 4:7-8 So humble yourselves before God. Resist the devil, and he will flee from you. 8 Come close to God, and God will come close to you. Wash your hands, you sinners; purify your hearts, for your loyalty is divided between God and the world.

Jonah 2:9 But I will offer sacrifices to you with songs of praise, and I will fulfill all my vows. For my salvation comes from the Lord alone.

Psalm 103:12 He has removed our sins as far from us as the east is from the west.

Isaiah 43:25 I—yes, I alone—will blot out your sins for my own sake and will never think of them again.

Isaiah 53:4-11 Yet it was our weaknesses he carried; it was our sorrows that weighed him down. And we thought his troubles were a punishment from God, a punishment for his own sins!

5 But he was pierced for our rebellion, crushed for our sins. He was beaten so we could be whole. He was whipped so we could be healed. 6 All of us, like sheep, have strayed away. We have left God's paths to follow our own. Yet the Lord laid on him the sins of us all.7 He was oppressed and treated harshly, yet he never said a word. He was led like a lamb to the slaughter. And as a sheep is silent before the shearers, he did not open his mouth. 8 Unjustly condemned, he was led away. No one cared that he died without descendants, that his life was cut short in midstream. But he was struck down for the rebellion of my people. 9 He had done no wrong and had never deceived anyone. But he was buried like a criminal; he was put in a rich man's grave.10 But it was the Lord's good plan to crush him and cause him grief. Yet when his life is made an offering for sin, he will have many descendants. He will enjoy a long life, and the Lord's good plan will prosper in his hands. 11 When he sees all that is accomplished by his anguish, he will be satisfied. And because of his experience, my righteous servant will make it possible for many to be counted righteous, for he will bear all their sins.

Colossians 1:21-23 This includes you who were once far away from God. You were his enemies, separated from him by your evil thoughts and actions. 22 Yet now he has reconciled you to himself through the death of Christ in his physical body. As a result, he has brought you into his own presence, and you are holy and blameless as you stand before him without a single fault. 23 But you must continue to believe this truth and stand firmly in it. Don't drift away from the assurance you received when you heard the Good News. The Good News has been preached all over the world, and I, Paul, have been appointed as God's servant to proclaim it.

Colossians 1:13-14 For he has rescued us from the kingdom of darkness and transferred us into the Kingdom of his dear Son, 14 who purchased our freedom[a] and forgave our sins.

Ephesians 1:7-14 He is so rich in kindness and grace that he purchased our freedom with the blood of his Son and forgave our sins. 8 He has showered his kindness on us, along with all wisdom and understanding. 9 God has now revealed to us his mysterious will regarding Christ—which is to fulfill his own good plan. 10 And this is the plan: At the right time he will bring everything together under the authority of Christ—everything in heaven and on earth. 11 Furthermore, because we are united with Christ, we have received an inheritance from God, for he chose us in advance, and he makes everything work out according to his plan. 12 God's purpose was that we Jews who were the first to trust in Christ would bring praise and glory to God. 13 And now you Gentiles have also heard the truth, the Good News that God saves you. And when you believed in Christ, he identified you as his own[b] by giving you the Holy Spirit, whom he promised long ago. 14 The Spirit is God's guarantee that he will give us the inheritance he promised and that he has purchased us to be his own people. He did this so we would praise and glorify him.

Psalm 23:4 Even when I walk through the darkest valley, I will not be afraid, for you are close beside me. Your rod and your staff protect and comfort me.

Hebrews 13:5b I will never fail you. I will never abandon you.

Joshua 1:5 No one will be able to stand against you as long as you live. For I will be with you as I was with Moses. I will not fail you or abandon you.

1 John 1:9 But if we confess our sins to him, he is faithful and just to forgive us our sins and to cleanse us from all wickedness.

Chapter Twelve

FOLLOWING THE RULES

NATHAN HAD ALWAYS BEEN good at taking direction. Early on his parents could see he was willing to follow rules. He was willing to do what they said. He respected them and he knew that they knew more than him. He was aware of their superior knowledge.

As Nathan grew and evolved, he did not sway from following that concept. He kept up with and did what he was asked. Seldom did he disobey or cause issues. He was a great kid! The kind every parent would want to have as a child.

Nathan explored, investigated, and fully lived life. The more he followed the advice and counsel of his parents, the more independence and freedom he was given. He could do most anything he wanted as long as it was within legal boundaries and within the guidelines of his parents. Nathan loved his life and how it was going. Seldom, if ever, did he ponder if things would be better if he demanded his own way in all capacities and opportunities. He just went along, realizing life was good. Even if he didn't get his way all the time. Or even if he could think of ways life would be better if he could do things a different way. He just went along and enjoyed what life brought him.

That type of life was foreign to many of his classmates in school.

The other kids kept goading him to act up and act out. They told Nathan about all the things they did against their parents. They shared with Nathan how things were hard but if they acted out, they could get what they wanted.

On several occasions Nathan asked the other kids if the result was worth all the emotional ordeal they went through. He asked if yelling, screaming, crying, tantrums, and getting upset was worth the result. The other kids sometimes said yes, but others just looked at him then walked away with their heads down. That convinced him that his way was the right way.

Nathan kept on being himself and living the way he thought best. Which was following the counsel of his parents. He came to recognize that his standards were unusual compared to other kids his age. He could feel the peer pressure. Yet he would not compromise. Inwardly he knew the other kids revered what he had. But they wouldn't allow themselves to come around.

Throughout his schooling he kept true to his belief. He had the best times with his parents. Family vacations were exceptional! The memories, oh the memories. Such wonderful times. He would not have traded them. His parents loved him and he loved them. It was such a harmonious relationship; an outsider would have not thought it possible.

Seldom was a voice raised in his house. Difficulties and situations were overcome together. Life was almost too good to be true. But yet it wasn't. It was true! There were hardships. Like his mother's miscarrying a baby. His dad turning down a different career position that would have caused the family to move to another state. Nathan understood that his dad did not take the job offer so that Nathan could stay at the school he attended.

While there were life wounds for Nathan, they were psychologically and emotionally bandaged, treated, and healed by his family unit. He was not left to deal with them on his own. His parents were always there for him.

Even though he didn't get the baby brother he always wanted, his life was still full and fulfilled. Love abounded because his dad, mom, and Nathan wanted to share the best of life together.

It seemed like his first eighteen years zoomed by. High school was soon over and it was time for him to step into college life. Leaving his parents behind and heading out was much harder than Nathan anticipated. He mourned and wept. He missed his parents immensely. His parents were the same. There were days they did not want to face the day without Nathan with them.

Over time, they all adjusted, even though life was not the same. Nathan went home as often as he could. His parents were there with open arms, beckoning him to come home more often. Come in. They wanted to know everything and he could not wait to catch up on his parents' lives. It seemed the weekends at home sped by at the speed of light. Soon he had to return to college.

One day at college, a cute chick came up to him as he was walking to class. She said a few words t h e n asked if she could walk with him. Nathan had never had a date or a girlfriend. He didn't really see a need. He was content with life as it was.

It wasn't that he was opposed to girls or thoughts of dating or even getting married. It just hadn't happened yet.

As they walked, the girl introduced herself. Jesse was a freshman like him. They discovered they didn't have any of the same classes though. As they were walking toward Nathan's next class, Jesse stopped and asked Nathan if he was a spiritual person. Nathan thought for a moment, as he had never contemplated that before. She was waiting for an answer. He had glanced away as he pondered. He looked back into her eyes and said that he wasn't sure. He said he had never really thought about it.

Jesse responded by asking him if he would like to find out. Nathan started feeling a bit uncomfortable. He wasn't sure why but he recognized that feeling. In his mind he seemed to take a long time to answer. Even though it was only seconds. He finally told Jesse that he guessed he would.

Jesse invited him to a meeting that night where he could find out more about being a spiritual person. Before she parted, she said it was a meeting of singing, listening, meditating, and praying. A time to learn about Jesus and being a spiritual person.

Nathan wasn't sure about going. He and his family never talked about being spiritual, or Jesus or God or anything like that. He remembered going to a church two times. Once for a funeral and the other for a wedding. He could not recall either his mom or dad making an influence in his life about God. It was just not discussed. He kind of knew it was out there but there were many of other interests and there was abiding love in his home. His family lived life together one day at a time. There was happiness.

That night, Nathan finished h is h homework by nine. Early enough to get to the meeting. He had pondered going or not going many times that day. Why go? Why not go? Maybe he could learn something. Maybe it would be boring and a drag. Ultimately, he decided to go so he could see Jesse again. At least that is what he told himself.

As he was going to the meeting, he felt himself becoming nervous. The kind of nervous that meant he was going to experience something out of his ordinary realm. Something was going down that night. Something that might change his life. Or it might just be something he needed to remove from his life.

When he arrived at the meeting, his first thoughts were that it was kind of like church but it was in a college class room. It was dark and the music was LOUD! He liked that. He didn't know where to sit and the only person he knew at all was Jesse. A guy came up to him and asked if he was meeting someone there. Nathan said he was meeting Jesse. The guy went and got her. She came to him, with a sweet smile on her face. She hugged him and said she was so glad he came. She led him to the front row as the music continued.

Nathan didn't know the songs but he swayed and watched the lyrics on the screen. He couldn't help but notice that Jesse knew the songs. She was singing along with her eyes closed and arms lifted toward something. He wasn't sure to what. He would have to ask her later.

While reading the lyrics to the songs, he noticed they concerned God and Jesus and a Holy Spirit. Nathan felt awkward and out of place. What had he gotten himself into? He wondered how long the event would last. He soon found out it had just begun and would go about 1½ hours.

The singing ended and a college-aged guy came up front and asked them to bow their heads and join him in prayer. Nathan bowed his head obediently. The guy said thanks to a God and to his son Jesus. Nathan found the prayer curious. The guy said Amen at the end of the prayer. Nathan wondered what that word meant.

They sat down. Nathan did not know what to expect. He glanced at Jesse. She smiled at him in such a way that he was glad he had sat down. His knees were weak and his heart palpitated. He felt his face flush. He remarked internally that this girl has a lot going for her and she is so lovely.

His thoughts were soon invaded by a middle-aged man coming to the front and started talking to the group. He said that he wanted to talk about how God has pursued each and every person on earth, including all of them at the meeting. Not one has missed seeing or experiencing him at some point in their lives. Everyone has had the opportunity to recognize it was God with them. Each human throughout history has engaged with God in some form or fashion. No matter who you are or where you have lived.

The middle-aged speaker went on to say that each of us had to make a decision upon that encounter. Either we turned to God and believed in Him or we turned away, hardened our hearts and went off to live for ourselves.

The speaker went on to say that once you experience God and turn away, God doesn't stop pursuing you. He wants you to ask Him to be your God. He wants you to be part of His family. A child of God. He said you can run but still God will come. He wants to take all that has happened in our life and then love you through those past things and all that will happen today and all that will happen in the future.

He went on, saying we have all sinned and come short of God's perfection and glory. But God wants to forgive us, yet we have to pay for our sins. The only way to pay for our sins is death. That is the penalty God requires. He has made that clear since the He first spoke to humans.

The speaker continued on saying that God, who loved us so very much, chose his one and only son to come down from heaven to earth. He chose him to live on earth and be God's living human being here on earth. God indicated in his Holy word, the Bible, that his son, named Jesus, would live out the sin penalty humans must pay. God loves people so much that he was willing to send his son down to earth to live, suffer, and die on a cross for our sins. The result of his death is that our sins are paid when we ask Jesus to be Our Savior and Lord. Then you will be radically freed and able to spend eternal life in heaven with God, Jesus, and the third part of the triune God who is named the Holy Spirit.

Then he said something very suspect. He said that after God allowed his son Jesus to be killed, he then arose from the grave after three days and now lives in heaven again. Jesus is there in heaven interceding for each believer every day. So that God will look at us through Jesus' sacrifice and see us as having our sin debt paid and are now perfect before him. Because and only because Jesus is perfect. So if God looks at us through Jesus' perfection then we are perfect before him.

Nathan wondered if that could be true. But he kept listening, finding himself intrigued by what the speaker was saying.

The speaker went on to say that while we remain here on earth we can live in peace and have the Holy Spirit counsel us spiritually. The Holy Spirit will convey the will and grace of God and the peace of love from Jesus. Yet if that is not enough God will bring you fulfillment and joy. When you ask Jesus to be your Savior and Lord, your eternal life with him begins at that instant.

You will still live on this earth for the remainder of your human days and face the tests of this sin-filled, depraved world, but God will lead you through each step of life.

In conclusion, the speaker asked if anyone at the meeting would like to join God's family and accept Jesus as their Savior. He asked anyone who wanted a life of liberty in Jesus Christ to stand and raise their hand.

Nathan felt a feeling he had not experienced before. He could sense an overcoming of love like he had never experienced before. He later came to understand that it was Jesus himself, imploring him to come and receive his love.

Slowly Nathan got to his feet and raised his hand. The speaker acknowledged his acceptance. Jesse reached over and squeezed his hand. Nathan felt a surge, a presence of a newness of beauty, joy, and love he had never experienced from his parents. A love beyond what humans can offer. He was overcome by emotions and tears of joy came spilling out.

The speaker asked those who accepted Jesus to come forward and receive a bit more information. Jesse asked if Nathan would like her to go with him. He was grateful and said yes. He was entering unknown territory and having a friend accompany him was comforting.

Following the instructions of how to find a Bible app, where to start reading, and introducing how to pray, the speaker invited them to be committed to God in all facets of life and return next week to the meeting. All of the new believers agreed to do so. Then the speaker asked them to get together with Jesse before the meeting the next week so she could guide them further. They all exchanged contact information and planned to meet with Jesse.

As they left the meeting room, Nathan felt that someone was accompanying him. A non-human. He felt an inner warmth like the sun warming his soul. Oh yes, he recalled, I now have the Holy Spirit spiritually directing me. That was a tremendously wonderful feeling.

Jesse was at his side. She asked Nathan if he wanted to hang out longer. He said no, that it was time to share the great news with his parents. But he did ask Jesse if they could meet the next day. With a very becoming smile, Jesse agreed. Something was percolating between them.

As Nathan walked away, he grabbed his phone and punched in his dad's number. His dad answered with their familiar love greeting. Nathan spoke rapidly and with joy that he had just been to a meeting where he discovered Jesus. He went on saying that he had accepted Jesus as his Savior and Lord.

His dad burst in screaming. "You did what?! You are now a Jesus boy? Do not ever come home again and do not ever call your mother or me again!" "CLICK!"

You as God

You are livid with anger at the dad and mom. You have put up with them for half a century with their self-founded belief system in themselves. You have been patient and waited for them to come to their senses. You made certain that they saw or heard instructors speak your message to believe in you. But they wouldn't.

Finally Nathan got it. He received you as God. Marvelous. Wonderful.

But those parents just tried to destroy his newfound belief. That's it.

I have given them enough time. They are going to hell tonight.

What God Does

There has been a huge party in heaven, celebrating those who received Jesus as their Savior and Lord that night. Including a celebration of Nathan's acceptance of Jesus, of course (Luke 15:6-8).

God sees the joy in Nathan's belief. He also knows the agony of suffering Nathan experiences at the hands of his dad (Psalm 2:3-6). The suffering from hi dad who just disowned him (Luke 12:51).

God sends messages through the Holy Spirit (John 14:26) to Nathan to reach out to Jesse. Nathan needs a rock of faith to lean on in the next hours and days. Nathan hears the Holy Spirit's pleas and calls Jesse who is willing to meet immediately and hear his experience.

When they meet, Nathan tells Jesse what happened. She is aghast. Nathan says he knows he can never let go of Jesus now and will live for him all of his days (Psalm 84:10). But how can he live without his family (Isaiah 41:10, Col. 2:6-8, John 14:27). Life revolved around his family.

God knows that Jesus brought a new life to people when he went to earth. He is fully aware that while he wants everyone to believe in Him and seek to be part of his family, not all will do so. Some will become hard-hearted and totally turn away and believe in whatever they can make up in their minds. The non-believers will say things and believe whatever their minds contrive so they will not have to accept Jesus as their Savior and Lord (Romans 1:28-32). Unfortunately, their unfulfilled lives on earth will end and they will spend eternity in hell. In hell there will be intense suffering, pain, and gnashing of teeth (Matthew 13:49-51). There will never be peace or happiness there. And it is for eternity.

God continues to send words of counsel to Jesse to console Nathan and pray over him. , which she does (2 Corinthians 1:3-5).

God is not going away; he is there for Nathan. His word, the Bible, and others will help him through this deep valley of despair. As Nathan deals with all the pain in the valley, he will slowly allow God to guide him and he will find a path back to level ground and then to climb a summit of spiritual experience with God, Jesus, and the Holy Spirit (Isaiah 26:3-4, Proverbs 3:5-6). It will be painful and hard but God's great hand of deliverance is on Nathan. It will happen. By trusting in God, Nathan will retain his joy of salvation even in the midst of this crushing loss of relationship (Isaiah 61:10). Through this time, Nathan will learn to pray and receive answered prayers from God (1 Thessalonians 5:16-18).

Jesus, while on earth, said that believing in him will bring divisions. Even divisions and broken relationships in families. He further encouraged believers that while there will be tribulations and trials in this world, His peace will be greater than the tribulations (John 16:33).

God continues to send messages to Nathan's dad and mom. He sends messages of his great love and that their lives will have the ultimate experience and unmitigated peace if they turn to him and accept Jesus as their Lord and Savior (2 Peter 3:9).

He won't stop sending those messages to them until they either break through to acceptance of Jesus or their lives on earth ends without them asking Jesus into their lives and they go to hell eternally.

God yearns to have Nathan's dad and mom come to faith and believe so that the family can be reunited. Nathan will lead them in faith if they will accept Jesus as their Savior and Lord. Together they can praise and bless Lord God Almighty, and have an even greater family bond than ever before.

Luke 15:6-7 When he arrives, he will call together his friends and neighbors, saying, Rejoice with me because I have found my lost sheep. 7 In the same way, there is more joy in heaven over one lost sinner who repents and returns to God than over ninety-nine others who are righteous and haven't strayed away!

Psalm 23:3-6 He renews my strength. He guides me along right paths, bringing honor to his name. 4 Even when I walk through the darkest valley, I will not be afraid, for you are close beside me. Your rod and your staff protect and comfort me. 5 You prepare a feast for me in the presence of my enemies. You honor me by anointing my head with oil. My cup overflows with blessings. 6 Surely your goodness and unfailing love will pursue me all the days of my life, and I will live in the house of the Lord forever.

Luke 12:31 Seek the Kingdom of God above all else, and he will give you everything you need.

John 14:26 But when the Father sends the Advocate as my representative—that is, the Holy Spirit—he will teach you everything and will remind you of everything I have told you.

Psalm 84:10 A single day in your courts is better than a thousand anywhere else! I would rather be a gatekeeper in the house of my God than live the good life in the homes of the wicked.

Isaiah 41:10 Don't be afraid, for I am with you. Don't be discouraged, for I am your God.

I will strengthen you and help you. I will hold you up with my victorious right hand.

Colossians 2:6-8 And now, just as you accepted Christ Jesus as your Lord, you must continue to follow him. 7 Let your roots grow down into him, and let your lives be built on him. Then your faith will grow strong in the truth you were taught, and you will overflow with thankfulness. 8 Don't let anyone capture you with empty philosophies and high-sounding nonsense that come from human thinking and from the spiritual powers[a] of this world, rather than from Christ.

John 14:27 I am leaving you with a gift—peace of mind and heart. And the peace I give is a gift the world cannot give. So don't be troubled or afraid.

Romans 1:28-32 Since they thought it foolish to acknowledge God, he abandoned them to their foolish thinking and let them do things that should never be done. 29 Their lives became full of every kind of wickedness, sin, greed, hate, envy, murder, quarreling, deception, malicious behavior, and gossip. 30 They are backstabbers, haters of God, insolent, proud, and boastful. They invent new ways of sinning, and they disobey their parents. 31 They refuse to understand, break their promises, are heartless, and have no mercy. 32 They know God's justice requires that those who do these things deserve to die, yet they do them anyway. Worse yet, they encourage others to do them, too.

Matthew 13:49-51 That is the way it will be at the end of the world. The angels will come and separate the wicked people from the righteous, 50 throwing the wicked into the fiery furnace, where there will be weeping and gnashing of teeth. 51 Do you understand all these things?

2 Corinthians 1:3-5 All praise to God, the Father of our Lord Jesus Christ. God is our merciful Father and the source of all comfort. 4 He comforts us in all our troubles so that we can comfort others. When they are troubled, we will be able to give them the same comfort God has given us. 5 For the more we suffer for Christ, the more God will shower us with his comfort through Christ.

Isaiah 26:3-4 You will keep in perfect peace all who trust in you, all whose thoughts are fixed on you! 4 Trust in the Lord always, for the Lord God is the eternal Rock.

Proverbs 3:5-6 Trust in the Lord with all your heart; do not depend on your own understanding. 6 Seek his will in all you do, and he will show you which path to take.

Isaiah 61:10 I am overwhelmed with joy in the Lord my God! For he has dressed me with the clothing of salvation and draped me in a robe of righteousness. I am like a bridegroom dressed for his wedding or a bride with her jewels.

1 Thessalonians 5:16-18 Always be joyful. 17 Never stop praying. 18 Be thankful in all circumstances, for this is God's will for you who belong to Christ

Jesus.

John 16:33 I have told you all this so that you may have peace in me. Here on earth, you will have many trials and sorrows. But take heart because I have overcome the world.

2 Peter 3:9 The Lord isn't really being slow about his promise, as some people think. No, he is being patient for your sake. He does not want anyone to be destroyed, but wants everyone to repent.

Chapter Thirteen

THE HATEFUL NEIGHBOR

L ET'S SAY YOU HAVE become God. You are the creator. You have made everything and everyone. All were created by your hand. You instruct them on how to live wisely. You let all people know how much you love them and how you want to interact in their lives daily. Initially, the people listen, hear, and enjoy.

A situation arises. A man, his wife, and four-year-old daughter live in a suburb. This family has a neighbor who is different. He doesn't really love anyone and is the fi rst to not love you. You, the creator god. The one who created him. He will not listen to you and does not care what you say or have written or is recorded about you. You send word to him that he needs to return to a life of following you. But he doesn't and he resolutely tells you where you can go.

He determines he hates the neighbors. Especially the little girl. She is an annoyance. Always making noise by singing to you. He wishes she were dead. He determines she must go, so he can live the kind of life he wants. A life he desires, without her annoying, disgusting singing to you.

You as the omniscient god see this all unfolding. So what do you do? You love this hateful neighbor man. You love the four-year-old daughter and her family. What should you do as god? Kill the hateful neighbor?

Then it hits you. Oh yeah, you have created everyone so that they have free will. They are allowed to do anything they want. Now you have a dilemma. The neighbor man wants the beautiful, charming four-year-old girl dead. You can foresee the devastation to the parents, the extended family, the community, and all who hear the news. They will want to kill the hateful neighbor. So what will you do?

Do you break your covenant promise and not allow free will anymore? Do you take out the hateful neighbor? Or do you allow him to go on with his plan?

Let's say you allow him to retain free will. He does the dreaded act and kills the four-year-old neighbor girl. In cold blood, with malice and is very happy she is dead. The parents of the girl are devastated. The girl's father wants revenge. He seeks justice. He demands it.

He screams at you, "Where are you in this whole thing, god (You)?" Even though the father knows it will never bring back his daughter, he wants justice. He looks at you. He looks at you in disgust. He decides he hates you because you did not stop the hateful neighbor man from killing his delightful daughter. Now he must spend all his days without his beautiful daughter. He hates you for letting it happen. He says to himself that he knows better than you. He screams, "What kind of god are you, that you will let my daughter die? I don't believe in you anymore. I hate you."

The father of the murdered four-year-old girl can't stand life anymore. All he can think about is how to get revenge on the neighbor man. He cannot get to him to take permanent physical revenge. Murdering the neighbor man consumes him. He thinks constantly about it. Yet he cannot get to him. That murderer.

Then a vile thought enters the father's mind. If he cannot get to the neighbor man; he can certainly take revenge upon his wife. She still lives next door. The father has even more premeditated thoughts. If he kills her then he will have revenge and the neighbor man will never have his wife back. He continues processing and likes the thought that the neighbor man will be in the same kind of agony he is in. His wife will be gone. She won't be able to call, write, or visit him in prison. He convinces himself that this plan will work perfectly. The neighbor man will never ever see or hear from his wife again.

Unbelievably, the father of the murdered girl completes the heinous act. He kills the neighbor's wife. He does not hide or conceal his guilt. He goes directly to the police and confesses his act.

The police take the father of the murdered four-year-old girl into custody. A trial takes place. The jury must decide if he should be killed because he did in fact maliciously kill the hateful neighbor's wife.

The neighbor's wife's family screams at you, god, in disgust that you let her murder happen. They now hate you and proclaim that no loving God would ever let that happen. They swear that they will never follow you again. With clenched fists and gnashing teeth, they spew that you are not a god of love.

In the meantime, the mother of the deceased four-year-old girl is left with no daughter and her husband is in jail. Most likely he is going to face the death penalty for killing the hateful neighbor's wife. She is beside herself. Sobbing, heartbroken, devastated. Wanting life to return to how it was. She realizes it never will and blames you and fully believes it is your fault. She sobs, blurting out the words that you could have stopped it. That you could have stopped all of it. She thoroughly believes you are a loathsome god. She screams that she hates you and will never follow you again. She develops an unchangeable mindset that she will do everything she can to turn everyone against you because you are not a god of love.

The father of the four-year-old is in jail. Waiting for his trial and sentence. He pleads with you to let him go and to be found justified for killing that hateful neighbor's wife. After all, the neighbor murdered his daughter. He pleads to you to answer his prayers and release him from a possible death sentence. He goes to trial, the jury realizes they must set a precedent so this will never happen again. Do they pray to you and seek your counsel? No. They believe they know best.

There are laws to handle this kind of thing. They do not need to seek you. The jury surmises the following things about you. If you had been a loving god, none of this would have happened. No way are they looking to you for anything ever again. They say that you aren't a loving god!

The jury convicts the father of the deceased four-year-old girl of murdering the neighbor's wife and hands him a death sentence.

The father of the murdered four-year-old girl goes on defaming you, declaring it is wrong, unjust, and unfair that he has been found guilty. In his cell he yells at the top of his lungs that you are not a god of love. He keeps repeating that you could have stopped all of it. He realizes he will not get to live out all his years with his wife. He doesn't hold back; he screams that he hates you. He declares all that repeatedly in interviews that are broadcast around the world.

The people of the world hear the father's interviews and declare it is wrong of you to have let that happen. You are not a god of love. They are certain they know better than you. They will take it from here. Many people say that maybe you created them, but they know better than the Creator. Because of these two murders, millions turn away from YOU and demand that you stay away from them. They know that they know better than you do.

If You Were God

Concerning the neighbor man, he is going to hell for murdering the little girl who loved you. No mercy for him. That's it, his fate is sealed.

The little girl is with you for eternity.

Now you have to decide about the little girl's father who killed the neighbor's wife. Are you going to justify his killing and not have him killed? Will you send him to Heaven or hell for eternity? Or, as God, are you going to let him off scot-free? Will you make it so he receives no punishment whatsoever? Is that fair? Is that right? You are God, and you get to make the call. You have to make a decision so people will return to you.

You hate the entire situation when the people you created put you in a situation when they succumb to hate and anger. You do not want to have to deal with it, and as God, you do not have to. You created people to serve and worship you. You are very tired of dealing with the whole situation. Why do people have to be so stupid? You need a break and a bit of space and time to decide what you want to do next. You ask yourself, when was the last time you had a vacation? All you want is a little peace and quiet, and you wonder how you can distance yourself from this situation.

However, there is still a massive clamoring on Earth being directed at you. They want you to take care of this matter. They pray that you will make a decision that is good for all to live by. You realize you need to set a standard, so this can never happen again.

What decision will you make about the father of the little girl who killed the neighbor's wife? You realize a decision must be made now because he killed the neighbor's wife in cold blood. Therefore, the father must be killed. You established that in your book of Counsel. Nobody is automatically doomed to hell or blessed with eternal life with you. You get to decide on who will make it into eternal life. Only you get to make that decision for each person based on their life, their choices, and what they did with their free will decisions. When they come to meet you at the end of their life, you will question them, and then you will decide where they will spend eternity.

There is no time for rest. You have to make a decision now. What decision will you make about the father of the little girl who killed the neighbor's wife? You weigh the circumstances again. He killed the neighbor's wife in cold blood. You determine the father of the little girl must die.

When he comes to meet you after his execution, you will question him, and then You will decide where he will spend eternity.

You reflect on when you created man and woman. You knew they must have a free will. You wanted them to have free will so they can worship you, serve you, and love you. When they are in accord with you they will understand your love for them. They will have a steadfast relationship with you. You cannot go back on your covenant promise of allowing all people to have free will! It is a forever covenant, yet you now are contemplating changing it. You are God and can change anything you want.

Will the people still love and follow you if you change something as vital to mankind's growth as free will? In a few generations the newly created won't know about the past when there was free will, since they won't have any. You will wipe it out of the history books. You will only have to endure the hate of the current living people. Once they are gone no one will have free will. You will decide everything. That sounds daunting, empty, and absent of all that makes your people special. But you also won't ever have to hear from the people that hate you ever again. You ponder that idea. You will decide about that soon.

On earth there remains a faithful minority who stay true to you and Your Ways. You select several throughout the generations to speak directly to them by Your Spirit. You call them Instructors. You speak into the Instructors' spirits. The core being of life. They take your words and convey them in writing, videos, in person, on social media, and through journalists to all people. Your book, Counsel, and Your instructions are spoken. The messages are repeatedly the same. "Return to you or you will send destruction, natural disasters, and mayhem will be allowed to prevail." You will send people who have never believed in you to overthrow, rule, and indenture all of you who once believed but have now turned away and are deliberately living away from you. Even those who remain faithful to you will have to endure these same things. Yet the faithful know that they will spend eternal life with you and that it will be glorious. Majestic and marvelous beyond belief.

By far the majority of people do not believe the Instructors you send. They do not believe you have the nerve to do that to them. They say repeatedly, with gnashing of their teeth, that you better not do that. No loving God would do that! If you truly are a loving God, You would never think of such a thing. Their foremost desire is that you will give them whatever they want. In providing abundantly for them in the past, they have misunderstood and taken the credit themselves for all the good that there is in their lives. Forgetting or ignoring that you provided all things for them. They have decided they want to be god of their own lives. Not wanting you to be their god. So they live that. Ignoring and defaming you whenever possible. Elevating themselves and living to honor themselves is now their life ambition.

You send some of the disasters you warned of. Some people are injured. Some die. There is destruction of homes and buildings, towns and cities. It takes them a long time to recover. Those who remain behind shake their fists at you and declare, "No god who loves us would do such a thing as you have done." They curse you and despise you. They turn even further away, rather than back toward you. They are incensed that they now have to do without certain things they want. The people affected have to take such effort to rebuild and restore. They wonder if life can ever return to the beautiful way it was. Because it is taking so long and because they do not have all their earthly benefits restored immediately, they blame you. They do not even consider that they need to return to you, love you, or worship you, their creator. Nor do they think of relationship restoration with you. Rather, they turn further away. They are vehemently angry with you. They know you don't love them or you would give them what they desire. A true and loving god would provide that. You would give them whatever is on their wish list because that is the only right thing to do. The created know better than you, their creator. They know what is best for them. The only time they speak of you is to curse you. When they think of you, it is with derision.

You think about eliminating free will once again. You are on the verge of eliminating it.

What God Does

God is love (1 John 4:8), forgiveness (1 John 1:9), justice (Psalm 37:28), and righteousness (Psalm 50:6). He lovingly created all people. He wants all people to realize His love for them. He also made decrees and a set of His laws for people to live by. People make laws for other people. God makes statutes for all people, at all times, for now and forever (Lev. 18:4-5).

God is creator of the universe and all people. He provides and provided so much to every one of us through His never-ending love. He loves to pour out His love on each of us. He also desires that we serve Him faithfully (Col. 3:23-25). The Lord will be with those who love Him. He will keep His promises (1 Kings 8:56-61).

Since He is God, He is also our judge. God's Word, the Holy Bible, says that a murderer shall be put to death upon conviction (Numbers 35:17).

God is also a forgiving Lord who will forgive all who come to Him, confessing in their hearts and with their mouths that they have sinned and confess what they have done against God and man (Romans 10:9-10). God will then forgive them and cleanse them from all unrighteousness. Forgiveness is available up to and including until your final breath.

That does not mean that the guilty will not have to pay the consequences and for the results of their actions done against mankind. Humankind will have set their standards. Some laws in some countries follow the statutes of God, While in other places the only governing laws are made by man. Those manmade laws are carried out upon the guilty.

God will and does forgive those who murder when they come seeking forgiveness from a repentant, humble, and honest heart. God will not accept a fake plea. He knows all. He is omniscient and omnipresent. He knows what everyone truly believes, thinks, and holds in his or her heart. God will not be fooled by those who hope they can trick God with fake belief.

There are examples in the Bible. Both Moses and David were forgiven for murderous acts. They both went on to serve the Lord, faithfully, because of their repentant hearts and a life-long commitment to love and serve the Lord.

God makes it clear that He is Lord and there is no other. He has established all the statutes and we need to live them out. However, when we do sin, He will not stay angry forever toward those who return to Him. But for the evil there will never be peace (Isaiah 57:16-21)

God created you to be with Him forever. Yet, if you turn away from Him and declare you do not want Him to be your God and that you do not believe He sent His one and only Son to earth to be Your Savior by Jesus Christ's suffering, death, and resurrection, He will ultimately accept your denial of Him and let you go to hell and spend eternity there. With no hope of ever leaving.

1 John 4:8 But anyone who does not love does not know God, for God is love.

1 John 1:9 But if we confess our sins to him, he is faithful and just to forgive us our sins and to cleanse us from all wickedness.

Psalm 37:28 For the Lord loves justice, and he will never abandon the godly. He will keep them safe forever, but the children of the wicked will die.

Psalm 50:6 Then let the heavens proclaim his justice, for God himself will be the judge.

Leviticus 18:4-5 You must obey all my regulations and be careful to obey my decrees, for I am the Lord your God. 5 If you obey my decrees and my regulations, you will find life through them. I am the Lord.

Colossians 3:23-25 Work willingly at whatever you do, as though you were working for the Lord rather than for people. 24 Remember that the Lord will give you an inheritance as your reward, and that the Master you are serving is Christ.[a] 25 But if you do what is wrong, you will be paid back for the wrong you have done. For God has no favorites.

1 Kings 8:56-61 Praise the Lord who has given rest to his people Israel, just as he promised. Not one word has failed of all the wonderful promises he gave through his servant Moses. 57 May the Lord our God be with us as he was with our ancestors; may he never leave us or abandon us. 58 May he give us the desire to do his will in everything and to obey all the commands, decrees, and regulations that he gave our ancestors. 59 And may these words that I have prayed in the presence of the Lord be before him constantly, day and night, so that the Lord our God may give justice to me and to his people of Israel, according to each day's needs. 60 Then people all over the earth will know that the Lord alone is God and there is no other. 61 And may you be completely faithful to the Lord our God. May you always obey his decrees and commands, just as you are doing today.

Numbers 35:17 Or if someone with a stone in his hand strikes and kills another person, it is murder, and the murderer must be put to death.

Romans 10:9 If you openly declare that Jesus is Lord and believe in your heart that God raised him from the dead, you will be saved.

Isaiah 57:16-21 For I will not fight against you forever; I will not always be angry. If I were, all people would pass away—all the souls I have made. 17 I was angry, so I punished these greedy people. I withdrew from them, but they kept going on their own stubborn way. 18 I have seen what they do, but I will heal them anyway! I will lead them. I will comfort those who mourn, 19 bringing words of praise to their lips. May they have abundant peace, both near and far, says the Lord, who heals them. 20 But those who still reject me are like the restless sea, which is never still but continually churns up mud and dirt. 21 There is no peace for the wicked, says my God.

Chapter Fourteen

THE INVESTOR

KEVIN HAD DONE PRETTY well for himself. He worked hard and had been devoted to his career He consistently saved for retirement. He had always wanted to have a luxurious retirement. His savings indicated he could live at a middleincome level. He would have to guard his spending and lifestyle. He did not like that thought or requirement. He wanted a life of true ease without limit. He had worked steadily and committed himself to his career. He told himself he deserved an easy going, care free life after his working days.

He had been through a divorce and that had hit his savings. But he was able to recover and live comfortably. Kevin wanted to get married again. Someday. Sooner rather than later. He was dating a woman he had fallen in love with and she seemed like the one. Val believed in a similar lifestyle and they were starting to plan a life together and a loving retirement.

The only problem, according to Kevin, is that Val did not have much in savings. Her husband had been a preacher. He died suddenly, leaving virtually no money to Val. He did not have life insurance or retirement savings as he made only a paltry income. She was receiving his pension benefis. But that was not much. Val had worked part-time but her projected social security benefits were minimal.

Kevin came to realize if they were going to get married and spend the rest of their life together, his retirement planning would have to carry the load. Following a meeting with his financial advisor, he was in a funk. His advisor had told him that the cost of supporting two in retirement meant living a reduced lifestyle at a lower level than Kevin desired.

That was really no surprise to Kevin. He anticipated that response. He loved Val and wanted her to be by his side for the rest of his days. She was younger and she should outlive him.

Yet, he could not let go of the desire to live at a higher level in retirement. Lower middle-income just wasn't for him. He started scouting around and looking into investments. He found information about a company that placed investors with startup companies.

Kevin thought about how an investment in a startup company could provide him the kind of return that would propel him to the lifestyle he wanted in retirement. He thought about a 500% return or more. That would do the trick. He hurriedly glossed over the high level of risk and greater-than-average potential for company failure than with established companies. Kevin was confident th at h e could sniff out the right startup company and by interviewing the company officers, he could determine whether they would be successful or not. He was ready to investigate further and to invest a good portion of his savings.

He projected that with a 500% return in four years, he and Val could live at the level he desired and he could then retire.

Val seemed much more wary than Kevin. She thought this could be a devastating loss for Kevin. Yet, she was committed to him. She also was completely aware that the money was his and he would have the ultimate say. She said little about the investment possibility, but she was sure Kevin could see that she thought it was too risky. She relayed to him she would be very content living on a moderate income and that being with him was enough. She did not need a grand lifestyle.

Kevin heard but he had his mind set on living at the level he always dreamed of living.

After a few weeks, the investment firm delivered an opportunity to Kevin. There was a startup biotech company that was researching and developing a product that would treat dementia in a whole new way. They were not yet approved for production, as the drug had not yet been approved by the Federal Drug Administration. The drug had not been through any of the four phases of clinical study.

However, the company's internal research indicated that they had developed a drug that decreased development of dementia. Early data had indicated that. The company needed more funding to be able to apply to the FDA and proceed with clinical trials.

Kevin was enamored by the concept. Plus, the company was in the city where he lived. He could drop by anytime and meet with them and stay current with progress. The investment company forewarned Kevin that only approximately 10-15% percent of developed drugs achieve approval by the FDA. That set Kevin on his heels. Yet he kept looking at the company's *pro forma* projections for revenue and profit once FDA approval was granted.

Kevin was consumed with the possibility of investing. He talked endlessly about it with Val. She listened but was not sold on the idea. He could see her uncertainty and kept providing her with reasons why it had to work. She remained skeptical, yet offered up her continued statement that it was his money. He should make the final decision.

Without a doubt Kevin knew it was his money. The decision would be his. He wanted that phenomenal return. He would be one of the fortunate ones who made a highrisk decision, and it paid off incredibly well. He would be the one others would envy because of the lifestyle he now lived in retirement. Only a few years from now he would be riding high.

He dreamed of his new lifestyle and taking Val places she had never thought of or dreamed about. She would love him even more for it.

The day came when he made the decision. He was so convinced, he invested one-half of his savings. He thought briefly about wh a t could happen if the venture failed. However, it was only a brief glance. He did not even talk with his financial advisor about calculating his projected retirement lifestyle if he lost all the investment.

He had to do it the investment. He just had to. This certainly had to work. Dementia was such a big deal that a solution would have astronomical returns in no time. Everyone was clamoring for a solution to dementia.

One Monday morning, he decided to do it. He called his financial advisor and had her sell one-half of his portfolio and wire transfer the money to the startup company's bank. The financial advisor tried to get him to wait until she could review the company and make a recommendation, but Kevin would not hear of it. His mind was made up. He told her she must do what he wanted done. The financial advisor knew she had to even though her senses said he should wait until she could review the company. Kevin wasn't willing to wait. He was ready now. So she complied, as she had no choice. It was Kevin's money and he had total control.

The investment is placed, and true to expectations, nothing appeared to be happening for six months or so. Kevin was starting to get impatient. He wanted to see some progress. He remained consumed with the company and having the drug approved. He made appointments and spoke with the company CEO several times. Each time the CEO reiterates they were on course.

A few agonizing months later, Kevin got the news that the company had gained approval to start clinical trials. He was informed that the company must achieve a high degree of success in diminishing the onset of dementia to move forward. Kevin was elated. He hardly heard the last words of necessary achievement. He was ecstatic about the progress. He immediately called Val, who congratulated the company and him. Kevin could still hear the reserve in her voice.

He told himself that yes, Val is correct. He should not be over the moon with only achieving an initial phase. Yet he couldn't help himself. He went back to being mesmerized by the idea of wealth.

The six-month trial originated. Kevin could hardly wait for results. He kept dreaming about the huge return and retiring even earlier than planned. In the meantime, his financial advisor called several times, inquiring about the investment and if he wanted her to perform some alternative retirement planning. He was having none of that. He was not far from hitting the big one... as they say. Val remained supportive and committed to Kevin. Their relationship went well when Kevin was not obsessed with the company's drug trial.

One day Kevin got a call from the company CEO. He explained to Kevin that the first-phase trials were going exceptionally well. The CEO went on to explain to Kevin that according to final projections the company would run short of money before the phase 4 trial was completed. He aske Kevin for another $100,000. Kevin said he would get back to him the next day. Tha t night Kevin pondered the situation. If the company could not get through all phases of clinical trials successfully, the company would either need to find another investor or investors, or they might fold and he will lose all his investment. Kevin had a sleepless night.

He didn't tell Val about the request. The next morning, he called and told the CEO to seek another investor. At the end of the conversation, Kevin stated that, "If you cannot find another investor, I will invest another $100,000." The CEO smiled as he hung up the phone, knowing he doesn't need to attempt to find another investor. All he has to do is call Kevin **back in a week** and explain that he could not find any other investors and that now would be a great time for Kevin to come through with the $100,000 investment.

That is how it played out. Kevin received the call and understood the CEO's statement. He knew he committed to the investment. So he called his financial advisor and requested the funds. Once again, his financial advisor, who was trying to look out for him, asked if he was going to make another high-risk investment. Kevin responded angrily that it was none of her business. That she should just do her job or he would move his account to a financial advisor who would follow his orders. The financial advisor agreed and said Kevin should move his account to another financial advisor.

Kevin wire transferred the money to the biotech company's bank account. But he was ill at ease. He couldn't readily explain it, but something didn't seem right. Val noticed a change in Kevin. He was acting differently. Anxious. Worried. Distant. Uninvolved. She asked several times. Kevin said everything would work out soon and then he could really enjoy life.

It was a Friday, like most Fridays. Kevin headed to work for an easier day than normal. His cell phone rang and, as it was a slower day at work, he took the call. It was the CEO of the biotech company. He called with news about the phase one clinical trial study. The words went off in Kevin's mind like a bomb. The test had failed. The company needed to return to research and development of the drug. The company needed more seed money to survive. The CEO asked if Kevin was willing to do that.

Kevin could barely say, "I will think about it." He took the rest of the day off. That did not help a bit. His very potential loss was all he could think about. What were the chances of getting his money back? Could he sue them for the money? He knew they didn't have money to continue. They did not have any revenue. They only had expenses. What now?

He drove through the city, getting more and more depressed. He decided he needed to tell Val. She would probably dump him. He thought that was what he deserved. Then he had another thought. Val was a Christian. She could pray to make a way that the company could give his money back. Yes, a good God who Val loved and Val said that God loves her. Kevin thought, "He will listen and make a way for me to get my money back."

He called Val and asked if he could immediately stop by. She agreed and Kevin drove directly to her condo. He thought of how the God who Val worshiped would be able to fix all this. He even thought that when You come through, he may start believing in You. But if You don't come through for him, he will never ever believe in You.

You as God

Kevin is stupidly gullible. Nobody should make those kinds of ridiculous mistakes. I am not helping him. Let him find his own way out of trouble. He will be broke his entire life. Even if he calls on me or Val intervenes and calls on me, I am not going to help him. He didn't listen to me or my helpers before, so I am not helping him now. Adios Kevin. Have the life of poverty you deserve, without Val by your side. You deserve what you get.

What God Does

God's love for Kevin never wavers Even though Kevin put money and hopes of an easy retirement life before God. In fact, God knew Kevin did not believe in him. Yet God remains there for Kevin if he will only turn to him, and ask Jesus (God's son) to be His Savior (Romans 5:10).

Once Kevin turns to God, repents of his sinful ways, and asks Jesus Christ to be his Savior, God will love him through all future events of his life. Even if there is failure and living with those accompanying results. If Kevin has success in many ways, including financial, God will gladly be his guide through all of that as well.

When Kevin lives for the Lord God instead of for himself, he will receive the benefit of the Holy Spirit leading him through all facets of life (John 14:26). We all need a Savior. We all need someone to guide us and help us at some point in our lives (2 Corinthians 7:6).

Romans 5:10 For since our friendship with God was restored by the death of his Son while we were still his enemies, we will certainly be saved through the life of his Son.

John 14:26 But when the Father sends the Advocate as my representative—that is, the Holy Spirit—he will teach you everything and will remind you of everything I have told you.

2 Corinthians 7:6 But God, who encourages those who are discouraged, encouraged us by the arrival of Titus.

Chapter Fifteen

I NEED A WIN

ROBERT LOOKS IN THE mirror and says that he just needs a win. He has been saying it for months. But now he is desperate, really desperate. There are not any outs. No ways to fi nagle around this one. His credit card accounts have been closed.

He has been the owner of a private plane/jet leasing business for over a decade. He had been uber-successful. The economy was good. Really good. He leased planes to companies to fl y their executives. He had many contacts in the business who owned planes and jets they wanted leased to get back part of their investment. The business was so lucrative that he himself bought a Learjet last year and started leasing it too. Well, actually financed 100% of it.

Last year he made over $3 million. He didn't fi le a tax return. He fell into the same game others in his industry practiced. That game says that once the IRS catches up with you, sales have been so good that you will just write a check to get them off your back. So he spent all $3m, plus more. Vacations galore. He bought a mammoth house with no money down. He loves driving crazy expensive sports cars. He leased them. His theory became who needs to own a car? He runs up $150k on credit cards. He loves having one $600 tequila after dinner each night. Well, now it has become more like two and sometimes three. He says it relaxes him greatly after a hard day of making deals. Robert thinks it doesn't get better than this. His wife Paula and their kids are living it up too. They are loving the life Robert has provided.

Then a recession hits. The greatest recession since the depression. Air travel plummets as does leasing of planes. He makes one sale in two years. He made a measly $10k last year. That doesn't even pay his car lease payments. He is losing his house. His wife can't be in her social circles. She screams at him to fix it. He can't. His kids want new clothes to keep up their lifestyle. In desperation he turns to God for the first time in his life and yells at God to give him a win. But none comes.

Not long after, his wife turns to God. Robert scoffs at the idea. He tells her that God didn't help him become successful. Why should he look to God now?

If God is so good, why won't He let Robert make a sale or twenty? Or why won't God let him get a job? Or why won't his wife get a job to help them through?

In disgust, Robert chastises himself for even thinking God could or would help. Besides, is there even a God?

However, nothing is happening other than Robert is stressed to the max, depressed, teetering on the edge of breakdown and starting to think that suicide is the only option left. He spends time, too much time, and every day, thinking of how to end his life. Paula will get the life insurance proceeds. That will get her through for four or five years. He thinks it could be his final gift to her and the kids.

Money is all they want anyway.

Ultimately, Robert comes to realize he doesn't have the courage to commit suicide. He is undecided about life after death. He has heard that people who commit suicide go to hell. But is there hell? He realizes Christians say they are going to heaven. But is there a heaven? He wonders where do good people go? What about reincarnation? Nah. He doesn't buy into that. What about nothing happening to your body, as there isn't really a life after death? He just goes to the dirt?

Robert doesn't really have any idea what will happen to him after death. He knows he can't and won't commit suicide until after he knows where he will go after he dies.

Robert also knows that he doesn't want to be remembered as suicidal. Yet, he can't see any other way out of this awful life he is living. He doesn't want to live another day. Not another moment. There are no answers.

No answers are coming from within. He realizes he has to make some decisions. Creditors are calling all the time. The bank is going to take back the house. The cars are going to be repossessed. He will get sued for all the credit card debt. The IRS has called and is demanding a meeting. There must be an answer. What could it be?

He has no idea. All he knows is that he is out of time.

Paula has been going to church for several months now. She has joined this women's fellowship group and seems to be building friendships. One night at a home fellowship meeting, she breaks down as the situation at home is just too overwhelming. She tells the group a little of the situation at home. Others in the group are going through some of the same thing, so they can sympathize. They promise their emotional support and show her in the Bible how God sees all believers through all things. Maybe it is a way through that is not ideal or what she hoped for but they assure her that God will see her through all things.

Paula is content and believes. She accepts that God will see her and Robert through this crisis. She realizes that with God she can face whatever takes place.

Others in home fellowship tell her of a Christian man who helps people with overwhelming financial difficulties. They know he has helped believers through some unbelievably difficult financial situations. Not that it was easy, but he helped them find a way through.

As the meeting ends, one of her new friends provides her the business contact information of the man. She whispers to Paula that he helped her through and taught her a lot about God.

That night, she asks Robert for a time for them to talk. They go to the patio. Robert can see a change in Paula's demeanor. She spills it all out to him. It takes a monumental effort, but he does not interrupt or scoff or belittle her. He doesn't believe it, but for some reason he is thankful that Paula believes.

Paula asks Robert to go with her to see this man. He cannot understand why he is nodding his head but for some unexplainable reason he agrees to go with his wife to a Christian financial counselor.

He regrets the decision almost immediately. But he is a man of his word. So he will go to one meeting.

Paula calls and sets the meeting date and time with Gerald. During the phone call, Gerald relays how the first meeting will go and what to expect. They determine that it will be best to meet at Gerald's house. He has a sense it will be easier for Robert to go there.

Paula is excited to go. Robert is repulsed with the idea. He knows this Gerald guy won't have any answers.

As they begin the meeting, Gerald says he will open with prayer and does so. Robert doesn't pray or interrupt. But he wants to tell Gerald off for praying, because he hates praying to a nobody.

Gerald begins tenderly and yet resolutely asking about their current situation and how it came to be. He asks specific questions so that there are no side stories that need to be told about the course of events. Paula immediately begins but she doesn't have the story right, so Robert breaks in and lays out the entire story. As he gets to the point of the business going south, he breaks down. The painful emotions come rolling out. Paula reaches for his hand. He sees she is crying as well. He tells all about spending more than they made, using credit for everything, and not paying the IRS. He doesn't leave out anything. He finally makes eye contact with Gerald who has been feverishly taking notes. Gerald had been nodding and saying "uh huh" and "hmmm" during Robert's story. Not once did Gerald express any negative attitude or interrupt with demeaning comments. He didn't interrupt at all.

Robert ended the story by saying he knows it is his fault and that there is no answer other than trying to scrape up enough money to go bankrupt, try to find a place to live, and attempt to start over.

That is when Gerald steps in and disagrees. He does not discount that Robert and Paula have made financial mistakes. But he doesn't emotionally pound them unmercifully either. He states this will take a lot of hard work and will take maximum effort on their parts. Not just once but many times.

He says that he has seen worse situations than theirs and all those people were able to overcome the problems and regain financial stability. They were all on the road to recovery and the worst was behind them.

Gerald stated he helped them through, but there was a lot of supreme effort the couples made. Gerald said they worked with him to create a Planned Spending Program (budget). He required them to live by it without exception. He said they did so and were paying back all creditors, were starting to save a bit of money, and were even giving a little money to the church because God saw them through the worst. Gerald said that even in the worst of it all, the couple fell deeper in love as they worked together to accomplish something they could not do on their own. It was God who helped them through.

Gerald gave the intake forms to Robert and Paula. He asked if they were ready to begin. He said they had to decide now. No more waiting. They couldn't take a month to decide. Things were too time sensitive. They had to start now. Robert wanted to think about it.

Paula wanted to start immediately. Gerald waited silently.

Robert finally agreed.

After he had reviewed the forms with them, Gerald scheduled the next meeting. He said they must bring all the financial information to the next meeting. The next meeting was in three days. Robert said that would be impossible. Gerald encouraged him and said he and Paula could do it, if they worked together. Gerald closed in prayer and asked if they were going to church on Sunday. He said he was visiting the church Paula was going to that Sunday. He was leading a remarriage class for couples. He said he hoped he would see them there. Robert wasn't willing to commit to attending.

That Sunday morning Robert woke up feeling he should go with Paula and the kids to church. It was a crazy feeling. Why would he have to go anyway? It had been a violently restless night of sleep. He got maybe a total of three hours of sleep. Yet, sometime during the night he fell asleep and awoke to that feeling. He sheepishly told Paula he wanted to go. She was elated.

After church they spotted Gerald. He was surrounded by people who were talking to him. After answering someone's question, for some reason, he looked away from the crowd of people around him and glanced at the patio. He spotted Robert and Paula and waved to them. Robert realized that wave meant more to him than the service.

That afternoon Robert and Paula went to work doing the assignment Gerald had given them. They had to figure out who they owed, the balance, minimum payments, interest rates, and contact information. The IRS had to be included in what they owed. In conclusion, it was a staggering amount of debt. Robert went into an emotional funk, thinking they could never find a way out. Paula tried to console him, saying Gerald must have an answer since he needed all that information.

At their next meeting, Robert observed how calm and at peace Gerald appeared. He wondered if Gerald could possibly have an answer. They reviewed all the data. Gerald did not look dismayed or point fingers of blame at them. He was working diligently Working to help them find solutions.

Robert wondered about what Gerald would be charging them for all the upcoming work. Gerald must have read his mind. He stopped for a moment and confirmed with them that he had created a non-profit organization where people make tax deductible gifts. The gifts were used for the help he gave others. He also reminded them that there were eight people in his organization. He supervised them all and so he would not be dealing only with Robert and Paula's difficulties. He let them know they would have to do some of heavy lifting themselves. Gerald would give those instructions and they had to do what he said. No compromises or procrastination were acceptable. Robert and Paula signed a form attesting to their commitment to do so.

Gerald told them that one or both of them had to get a job. Gerald said he was working like crazy to make any airline lease transaction happen. Paula said she could apply for a marketing rep job she heard of, but it only paid commission. Gerald said she should apply.

Gerald also encouraged Robert to think beyond his closedminded realm of what else he could do in the air transportation industry or in another industry. It suddenly dawned on Robert that he knew numerous airplane owners who started diversifying by investing in rental properties. Those new owners did not want to manage the properties. They all used property managers. Robert pondered the possibility of becoming a property manager. Gerald told him to do it. So that day, Robert started making contacts.

Gerald helped them build a Planned Spending Program (budget) at the meeting. It took a substantial amount of time.

The first expense line was Giving and Tithing. Gerald said directly to Paula "Since you are now a believer, and you love Jesus, you should give him something each time you make money." He referenced Deuteronomy 8:18 where it says God gave us the ability to make wealth. Gerald suggested that the first money she made and each time she made money, she should give 25 cents to the church. With tears flowing, she willingly accepted the opportunity. She said she did love Jesus and wanted the church to be able to stay open, especially during the recession. Robert thought it was a stupid idea but didn't say anything. Gerald could read Robert's mind and just nodded once at him after Paula's affirmation. Then Gerald said Robert should consider the same principle.

Next, they reviewed the house and Gerald told them they would need to move. They should seek approval from the mortgage company to do a short sale. Before Robert could blurt out the question of where they will move, Gerald stated that he should check with his clients and friends to see what they could do to rent them a place. Robert reluctantly agreed, even though that meant he would need to tell them of his failure and at least partially about his mistakes.

Gerald saw they had about eight thousand dollars in the bank. He said they should take five thousand dollars and buy the very best-looking older car they could find. He said it would keep the level of status Robert wanted to keep. A highquality car could do that. He recommended some brands that included Mercedes, Land Rover, Cadillac, BMW, Infiniti and Lexus, which Robert could drive when he met with jet leasing prospects.

Then he said to voluntarily return the two cars they have leases on to the bank. A voluntary repossession would not look as bad on their credit report as an involuntary repossession. Robert and Paula said they would buy a five thousand dollar car and turn in the other two.

Gerald thanked them for making that hard decision. Then he informed them that based upon the Planned Spending Program they created, they would be able to pay a certain amount to each credit card company every month. They would need to call each credit card company, ask for the collection or fraud manager, and seek grace and mercy. Asking for grace and mercy to waive or reduce interest and make smaller than minimum payments. Gerald provided them with a printout of exact words to say, including thanking the credit card company for their extreme grace in working with them.

Further, Gerald said that he would go with them to a meeting with the IRS. There was an office in the city, and they had to make an appointment. He would free up his schedule to be there. He said would present their financial situation to the IRS agent and inform agents through their final budget what they could possibly pay.

They would need a long-term workout, which included interest, but Gerald said there was a good chance it could happen.

That was a monumental, life-changing meeting. At the end, Gerald prayed for Robert and Paula by name and asked God to give them courage, conviction, ability, and peace to accomplish all they needed to accomplish before their next meeting, one week from today. Gerald also said he would be praying for them every day to rely on Jesus and to have the ability to accomplish all they needed to do.

On the drive home, Robert and Paula both said how they had to do what Gerald said, yet both were scared and stressed about doing it. They committed to be a team and do it together. Paula reached over and gave Robert a squeeze on his hand as he continued driving. She whispered that they could do it and she was with him for ever and ever. Suddenly, Robert could no longer hold back the tears and he thanked her from the wellspring of his heart. Mumbling "yes, they can do it".

The next week was a flurry of activity for Robert and Paula. Robert met with the bank and after four days of providing information and discussions, the mortgage officer was able to approve them selling the house on a short sale. The house went up for sale the next day.

Paula applied for and was accepted for the marketing rep job. She would need to start the following Monday. She was elated but still wondered if she could make a living in marketing.

Robert talked to a good friend who had a rental house available. He told the friend the truth. The friend agreed to rent the house to them at a reduced rate. He couldn't believe how things were going their way.

However, at home, the kids were not happy. Life was going to change for them too and they did not like it. Robert and Paula spoke as lovingly and positively as they could. They let the kids know they would be changing schools once they moved and they would be able to start over with new friends. No longer would they have uppity friends who expected them to live a certain way. Hopefully now, they would be without social pressure from classmates. The kids didn't like it but what choice did they have? They seemed to accept it.

Robert and Paula split up calling the credit card companies. Paula had better negotiating success than Robert, but in the end some form of compromise was made on all the credit card accounts. They both let out a huge sigh of relief when those phone calls were completed and plans were in place. Each call took over thirty minutes, waiting, talking, and sometimes getting transferred endlessly. They always asked for mercy and grace, stating to each company that they were going to repay the debt.

The following day, Robert called some of his air leasing clients who owned rental units and conversed about a property management company he formed. He stated how he could manage for less as it was going to be run by him and his wife. Hardly no overhead expenses. To his surprise, within two days he had become the property manager of four rental properties. Not large complexes, but each property was at least four units. He thought he did a good job. He successfully became the property manager of four properties. He had only made thirteen phone calls. He thought he might be good at something after all.

They started looking for cars but couldn't come up with any right away, so they held on to the leased cars.

Sunday came and the family went to church again. Robert listened to the message this time and heard the pastor talk of how everyone, at some point in their lives, needed support of some kind. He heard that no one can do all of life on their own. Support was needed from someone greater than a human. He heard the pastor talk of Jesus, who was ready and willing to have all people come to him and lay down their heavy burdens. Once they did, Jesus would be their Savior and never-ending resource of help and support throughout their lives.

Robert wondered if that was really what he needed.

Later that day, he talked with Paula. He asked if she thought the pastor was right. He also wondered if she thought Gerald was praying for them every day. Paula gazed into his eyes. She slowly and softly affirmed that she believed that the pastor was correct, and Gerald was praying for them every day, just as he said. She added that she was praying for Robert, herself, and the kids as well. Many times, every day. Robert marveled at that.

The day of the meeting with Gerald arrived. They went to his office and were beaming about the progress they had made. They relayed the unbelievably good news. Gerald joined in their rejoicing. He repeatedly told them how proud he was of them and the work they had done.

He suddenly stopped and asked Robert if he thought they had the ability to accomplish all that was done on their own or did he think they had a spiritual helper. Paula's eyes welled up with tears. She knew the answer. Robert glanced away and said that as much as he wished it was all done by themselves, there just had to be a spiritual helper. Gerald agreed and said that he was praying for it to happen just that way.

Suddenly Robert was overcome with emotion as he recognized that this Jesus guy must have been helping them through all of those difficult times in the past week. He wanted Jesus with him. Both now and forever. He said that to Gerald and Paula. Gerald gave a smile of assurance and led Robert in a salvation prayer. He told Robert that he would never be alone again. Especially when hard times come and he does not know where to turn or what to do. Robert acknowledged that.

Robert and Paula embraced, and Robert felt her deep abiding love.

Before concluding, they made a call to the IRS, which they had not done in the last week. A meeting was set, and Gerald was going with them. While Robert and Paula were still scared about that meeting, they knew that Gerald was going with them, and Jesus was too.

If You Were God

Robert, I gave you so much talent and ability. You used it for your good. Never thinking of me or how I made it possible for you. You didn't even recognize I created you. I gave you the understanding to know that. But you stepped right past it and congratulated yourself on your successes. It really ticks me off. Never once did you offer up a thank you to me. Instead, you ignored my existence and heaped praise all over yourself.

You even thought you could get away with being financially irresponsible because of your great abilities. Well, you didn't. I made sure of that. You got what everyone else who goes against me gets. A life ruined.

Now you can pay the consequences of all you did by ignoring me and living only for yourself. It will take the rest of your life to clean this up. Maybe you will never recover. Do you think Paula and the kids will stay with you after the mess you made? Made all in the name of glorious Robert the genius.

Hah, I am not even wishing you good luck. You're on your own. If you ever turn to me, I will listen, I guess. But you will still have to work everything out on your own because you didn't honor me with the success I granted you.

Paula, I am glad you finally came to your senses and turned to me. But you also, for the longest time, were just interested in getting ahead and being socially superior to everyone else. You will have to pay for that with humility and living a much lower lifestyle. However, since you figured out your mistakes and turned back to me on your own, I rethought if I wanted you to be with me or not. I have decided I am here with you for the future. But you will have to live with your mistakes!

What God Does

Robert, my son, how good of you to come to me, at last. Welcome to my family. We both know you lived without me for a long, long time.

You thought you were successful all on your own, but I was blessing you by creating you with a mind to succeed at the career you chose. I was there with you before you were formed (Psalm 139:15).

You were just like many others who I created. They and you were endowed with ability, creativity, and dreams. Unfortunately, many of you sought to live life your way and I did nothing to stop you. However, I did send counsel through the Bible and by believers who compassionately cared about your soul and wanted you to receive my only Son, Jesus, as your Savior, and know that you have eternal life secured with me in heaven.

Sadly, many, including yourself, did not take that opportunity, but instead were bent on living only for themselves and their successes. Not just financial success, but also power, prestige, and honor. Along with other things.

I am a jealous God (Exodus 34:14), but jealous my way, not like you are jealous.

I created you to know of my love and return it with devotion. But you would not. I decided to send a way for you to return. So, for many of you, it was necessary that I let you fail so you would consider me again. You had heard of me and knew about me, but you scoffed at the notion of needing a Savior. Your thinking was who needs a God who you could turn to and pray to that would help you every step of the way? It saddened my heart that you and others would not listen. I had to allow you to go your own way (Romans 1:21-23).

I am thankful, Robert, that somehow my message broke through to you even though you did not know my words in the Bible. So you may know them now, here are words that I had the prophet Zechariah write in Zechariah 1:3, Return to Me, declares the Lord of hosts, and I shall return to you.

Now you know that when you were in desperation and opened your heart to me, and sought me with all your soul (Deuteronomy 4:29), I came to you and accepted you into my family, once and forever. Jesus is now your Savior, just as you asked Him to be (1 John 4:16, 1 John 5:11). You are part of my family (Ephesians 1:14) from now throughout eternity.

Come continually to me, Robert. There are many things remaining to resolve about your former life. You will need hope and my compassionate love to see you through. The consequences of life will need to be faced and resolved, but I will be by your side, guiding you through. Directing you each step of the way. I will never leave you (Hebrews 13:5).

From this moment, be diligent to be an approved worker for me and I will help you handle the word of truth (2 Timothy 2:15) with honor and you will be my disciple, wherever you go and whatever you do.

Press on toward the goal of an abundant life with me forever and ever. Forget what is behind and cling to what lies ahead (Philippians 3:13-14).

I am asking that you be devoted to me all your days. Doing missional work from Me and my kingdom. Bringing lost souls to the cross of Jesus to receive salvation.

Your story will have a mighty influence on others. While your failure may be a source of great angst for you now, it is a God story for you to tell people. When you include human failure with God's restoration and love when you did not deserve it, you will influence many, many people (Acts 1:8b).

You and Paula still have things to accomplish to get stabilized but start today living on the solid foundation of salvation that I provide (Luke 6:48). I will move mountains of difficulties (Luke 18:27b) as you remain faithful to me. I am able, powerful, and mighty. There is no other like me (Isaiah 46:9).

My love for you will never end. I am with you now and always, in every way. Helping you through all things. I am always on the move (Isaiah 43:19). I am moving you by the power of the Holy Spirit who only communes and communicates with those who love me and My Son Jesus Christ.

Always lean into me and seek my counsel.W e will make it through all things together (Job 42:2, Philippians 4:13).

Deuteronomy 8:18 Remember the Lord your God. He is the one who gives you power to be successful, in order to fulfill the covenant he confirmed to your ancestors with an oath.

Psalm 139:15 You watched me as I was being formed in utter seclusion, as I was woven together in the dark of the womb.

Exodus 34:14 You must worship no other gods, for the Lord, whose very name is Jealous, is a God who is jealous about his relationship with you.

Romans 1:21-23 Yes, they knew God, but they wouldn't worship him as God or even give him thanks. And they began to think up foolish ideas of what God was like. As a result, their minds became dark and confused. 22 Claiming to be wise, they instead became utter fools. 23 And instead of worshiping the glorious, everliving God, they worshiped idols made to look like mere people and birds and animals and reptiles.

Zechariah 1:3 Therefore, say to the people, This is what the Lord of Heaven's Armies says: Return to me, and I will return to you, says the Lord of Heaven's Armies.

Deuteronomy 4:29 But from there you will search again for the Lord your God. And if you search for him with all your heart and soul, you will find him.

1 John 4:16 We know how much God loves us, and we have put our trust in his love. God is love, and all who live in love, live in God, and God lives in them.

1.**John 5:11** And this is what God has testified: He has given us eternal life, and this life is in his Son.

Ephesians 1:14 The Spirit is God's guarantee that he will give us the inheritance he promised and that he has purchased us to be his own people. He did this so we would praise and glorify him.

Hebrews 13:5b I will never fail you. I will never abandon you.

1. **Timothy 2:15** Work hard so you can present yourself to God and receive his approval. Be a good worker, one who does not need to be ashamed and who correctly explains the word of truth.

Philippians 3:13-14 No, dear brothers and sisters, I have not achieved it,[a] but I focus on this one thing: Forgetting the past and looking forward to what lies ahead, 14 I press on to reach the end of the race and receive the heavenly prize for which God, through Christ Jesus, is calling us.

Luke 6:48 It is like a person building a house who digs deep and lays the foundation on solid rock. When the floodwaters rise and break against that house, it stands firm because it is well built.

Luke 18:27 He replied,W hat is impossible for people is possible with God.

Isaiah 46:9 Remember the things I have done in the past. For I alone am God! I am God, and there is none like me.

Isaiah 43:19 For I am about to do something new. See, I have already begun! Do you not see it? I will make a pathway through the wilderness. I will create rivers in the dry wasteland.

Job 42:2 I know that you can do anything, and no one can stop you.

Philippians 4:13 For I can do everything through Christ, who gives me strength.

Chapter Sixteen

THE MUSICIANS

THE THREE OF THEM had formed a music group. Had a couple of hits. Were on the road a lot. Got along okay. Two guys, Jordan and Aaron. One girl, Gracie. All married to other people.

While on the road, Aaron and Gracie would hook up. They can't get enough of each other. Jordan is angry with them. But not like they can't do their thing. It was just interfering with their old way of life.

As time goes on, they get stuck musically and can't craft any songs. The new stuff sounds just like the old stuff. The music company isn't happy. They may get their contract revoked if they don't create music. They are working feverishly to write new songs, but the creativity is gone.

In desperation they decide to turn away from drugs, debauchery (except the affair), Buddhism, and try God. But still nothing comes.

What kind of God would deny them?

Then the devastating news hits. Spouses fi nd out about the affair. On top of that, Gracie discovers she is pregnant. What now?

The spouses team up and say they are going to make public announcements. Aaron and Gracie are fraught with fear of their fans and family finding out. They try to appease their soon to be ex-spouses but nothing works. They are doomed.Gracie and Aaron have several long conversations, about them and the baby. They had spent almost ten years together on the road, before the affair started. They both had admitted they had sixted each other from the start. Each of them conveyed how they tried little things to see if the other was interested but when the bait wasn't taken, they both decided it was not to be and they would just be great friends and killer musicians.

Along the way, both Gracie and Aaron had each found someone they could love, enjoy, and build a life together. They both called it love and meant it. When they weren't on the road or in the recording studio, they gave themselves to their marriages. Aaron and Gracie thought the marriages were good, but both thought there could be more to love. Whenever they spent time around each other, they asked themselves why their feelings for their mates were not the same as the soul connection they had with each other.

On the night it went down, neither had planned anything. It was just another night of travel and they were on the bus. They both had showered and felt refreshed. Jordan had knocked off early as he was fighting a cold.

Aaron saw Gracie and immediately thought she looked stunning. She had on new jammies and he could tell she didn't have a bra on. He wondered if she was wearing panties. She was wearing her hair a little different. It was slightly wet. He loved it. He could feel the lust burning in his body.

Gracie took one look at Aaron wearing only jeans and no shirt. She was captivated. She didn't know if she could control herself. She had wanted Aaron for so long. She wondered if this could be the night.

They both started small talk as usual, but both were thinking about doing it. Thoughts also came to mind, for each of them, of their spouses. They both set those thoughts and feelings aside and went back to focusing on each other. The passion was overflowing and both could tell that the other wanted to be in the other's arms.

Aaron came and sat by Gracie, tenderly put his arm around her, drew her near and kissed her sweetly and passionately. That was how it all started. They immersed themselves into the other and they continued. Having sex, then collapsing in each other's arms. They awoke to Jordan saying, "What the...?"

They did not try to hide anything from Jordan. Words came spilling out of both Aaron and Gracie. It became obvious to Jordan that they both really were in love with the other and had been for quite some time. He wondered how he could have missed it.

Jordan tried his best to accept Aaron's and Gracie new love affair. But he couldn't divert his mind from the fact that he knew both of their spouses and he cared for both of them. He knew all four of those people, whom he loved and cared for, were going to get hurt, very deeply. None of their lives will ever be the same again. In his heart, he mourned for each of them as the disastrous news had to come out. Most likely in an unexpected way. He wished he could just slink away.

Aaron and Gracie could not stop living, loving, and touching each other. They immersed themselves into each other. Conversations with their mates were most difficult though. They both attempted to live the part of being faithful spouses. Yet their hearts were not in it.

They both dreaded when the tour ended and they would go home to their mates. So in the meantime they took advantage of every opportunity they had. Of course, all the roadies came to know about the affair, as did their manager and others who saw them on the road.

The day that the tour ended came way too soon for both Gracie and Aaron. They parted after sharing one last intimate time together. It was hard to imagine how they would go on without spending every day together.

They were both greeted by their loving spouses, eager to spend time together. Of course, that meant every form of passion that they previously enjoyed. Naturally, intimate time was the first thing. Both Gracie and Aaron made it through that by thinking of the other.

Later that evening, both spouses sensed a change in their mates. Each spouses hoped it was just readjustment from being on the road so long. But the change didn't abate.

Aaron and Gracie managed to go three days without texting or seeing other. Both were hurting and miserable. Both were sad and dismayed that they no longer loved their mates as before. Both of them were wondering how they would break it with them.

Even though Gracie and Aaron had not talked about it, they both knew they were going to be together for life.

Jordan was all mixed up about what to do about the band and Gracie and Aaron. He loved them both, but had not conceived there would be an affair. He liked their spouses too. They had a record contract, which they needed to fulfill.

He pondered, questioned, and let it play over in his mind. Could he go on musically and as close friends with Gracie and Aaron? He just couldn't reach a conclusion. It was messing with his head and psyche.

Finally, he decided to not make any decision at this point. He would wait for what happens now that they are all back at their homes. But in the meantime, their manager has been calling.

The record company wants them in the studio recording a new EP.

Jordan couldn't imagine being creative with all the upheaval going on.

Several more days went by when Aaron received his first text from Gracie. The text contained just two words, which threw his and her lives into an overwhelming gut-wrenching, lifealtering, heart-shaking spiral. Gracie had texted, "I'm pregnant."

If You Were God

Idiots. Aaron and Gracie, you are complete idiots. Stupid beyond belief. Why couldn't you hold your lust under control? I gave you both great spouses. Happy families. Look at things now. You ruined everything.

I gave you success and privilege.W hen I created you with musical gifts, it was meant to be used so you could advance music for the purpose of worshiping me and drawing others to me. But no, you wouldn't stay committed to me.Y ou gave into your lustful selves.

You are on your own now. Find your own way!

As for the spouses. I am here for them. Please come to me. I will guide you and help you.

Jordan, get away from Gracie and Aaron as fast as you can.

What God Does

Aaron and Gracie, I am so saddened that you have left your spouses and me behind. My Word, the Holy Bible, has given you instructions to live by. How I wish you would have heeded my counsel of how to escape temptation (1 Cor. 10:13). You should have run from each other in order to keep your marriages intact.

Yes, I do understand how temptation can be overwhelmingly alluring. I sent my Son, Jesus Christ, to earth to save all sinners. While there, he encountered every type of temptation known to humanity. Yet he did not sin (Hebrews 4:15).

Life is going to become a travesty for both of you. While it is, I will be available for counsel (Psalm 50:15). My Word, the Holy Bible, can direct you in ways to live (John 14:23, Colossians 1:21-23). Once you seek me, my counsel, and live for me, I will be your guide and counsel all your days if you live for me and love me in return (Ephesians 5:17, 1 John 4:19).

You will have to endure decisions you do not want to make. Divorce is imminent. Your spouses will experience great pain because of your affair. They may hate you. Who knows if your fans will accept you and your music again? Jordan will need to make a decision too.

People are going to judge you (James 4:11-12) and it will last a lifetime. Some will support you and come along beside you. I am the one true judge. The only judge that matters. Abide in me and I will also abide in you. I will not leave you if your love remains in me.

Jordan, come to me, I will give you rest, solace, and comfort (Matt. 11:28). Seek me for answers, I will provide them when you seek me with your whole heart (Jer. 33:3). You will need someone to sustain and walk with you (Eccl. 4:9-10). If you decide to remain with Aaron and Gracie, be a significant influence and lead them back to me through your example (James 5:20). But first, come rest, regain your emotional and psychological strength. Wait until the time is right to move forward (Psalm 27:11).

1 Corinthians 10:13 The temptations in your life are no different from what others experience. And God is faithful. He will not allow the temptation to be more than you can stand. When you are tempted, he will show you a way out so that you can endure.

Hebrews 4:15 This High Priest of ours understands our weaknesses, for he faced all of the same testing we do, yet he did not sin.

Psalm 50:15 Then call on me when you are in trouble, and I will rescue you, and you will give me glory.

John 14:23 Jesus replied, All who love me will do what I say. My Father will love them, and we will come and make our home with each of them.

Colossians 1:21-23 This includes you who were once far away from God. You were his enemies, separated from him by your evil thoughts and actions. 22 Yet now he has reconciled you to himself through the death of Christ in his physical body. As a result, he has brought you into his own presence, and you are holy and blameless as you stand before him without a single fault. 23 But you must continue to believe this truth and stand firmly in it. Don't drift away from the assurance you received when you heard the Good News. The Good News has been preached all over the world, and I, Paul, have been appointed as God's servant to proclaim it.

Ephesians 5:17 Don't act thoughtlessly, but understand what the Lord wants you to do.

1 John 4:19 We love each other[a] because he loved us first.

James 4: 11-12 Don't speak evil against each other, dear brothers and sisters.[a] If you criticize and judge each other, then you are criticizing and judging God's law. But your job is to obey the law, not to judge whether it applies to you. 12 God alone, who gave the law, is the Judge. He alone has the power to save or to destroy. So what right do you have to judge your neighbor?

Matthew 11:28 Then Jesus said, Come to me, all of you who are weary and carry heavy burdens, and I will give you rest.

Jeremiah 33:3 Ask me and I will tell you remarkable secrets you do not know about things to come.

Ecclesiastes 4:9-10 Two people are better off than one, for they can help each other succeed. 10 If one person falls, the other can reach out and help. But someone who falls alone is in real trouble.

James 5:20 You can be sure that whoever brings the sinner back from wandering will save that person from death and bring about the forgiveness of many sins.

Psalm 27:11 Wait patiently for the Lord. Be brave and courageous.
Yes, wait patiently for the Lord.

Chapter Seventeen

A FINAL LOOK

WAY TO GO, YOU made it this far. You have read, seen, and internalized how we defi ned stories and described scenarios of you as God. I relayed what God's Word is in the Bible and how every experience you have or thoughts you never voice can be heard, interpreted, and acted on by God. That is because God is God.

By now, you may also be saying I did not do a good job when I portrayed you as God running the world. As there are billions of people in this world, there are probably millions of different styles, intensities, and interpretations when you were being God. If you were the Big Kahuna, you may run the universe your way, making the world a better place.

However, if you took a deeper look at your decisions when you were God, you might fi nd that when you decided to help some people, there was another one or others you could help.

Did you fi nd out that millions of people want the opportunity to have it their way by being God just like your same desire? So, in the end, when you were God, did you make the right decisions?

A vast amount of people want the opportunity to be God because they think they would do it better than the real, true, living God. They think that if they were God and in control, the world would be more humane, healthy, and kind. They tell themselves they would finally have complete control over everything by being God. Because life hasn't been fair. Does that make it so you deserve to be God?

Unfortunately, all humans are finite, and we have expiration dates. We cannot make ourselves eternal no matter how much we want it to happen. God is the ONLY eternal being. He lives in all ways—continually! He exists not just for our short life span but for all times, spanning the lifetimes of all the people throughout the world.

A considerable number of you want absolute control over everything in your life and even the world. You think you know better than the only living God. You convince yourself that you will lead people better and treat everyone, fairly regardless of the circumstances. You think that, as God, you will always do what is right for all people.

However, as you have read in previous chapters, even if you are God, you will not be able to provide everyone with what they want in life. After reading all the pages, you may finally recognize that many people only look out for *numero uno*. If you were God and did not give everyone what they prayed for, you have come to recognize that they will turn away from you. They may even begin to believe in another God or entity. They may even come to despise you. Some will fall away from you and start to believe in only themselves. If you are God, what will you do? How will you handle those who refuse to believe in you anymore?

If you are God for a day, an hour, or longer, you will find that with every decision you make, there will always be some you could not please. So perhaps you think the best answer is only to make decisions that please you as God. But as God, if you do as you please, then you will offend many. The people who pray to you and do not receive what they want will take affront against you. They will take offense because you did NOT give them what they wanted.

Perhaps now you see that being God as a human is an impossibility. You now understand that you will never be able to be God. No matter how you desire to be God, it can never happen.

However, in the quiet moments of your thoughts, there is good news for you if you believe in God.

God is your God. God lovingly waits for you to surrender yourself to Him. God wants you to experience earthly and eternal life with Him through His Son, Jesus Christ, Savior of the world.

Now that you have read this book, today is YOUR day! You have a God who loves you and is seeking a deep abiding relationship with you. He is waiting for you. God longs for you to turn to Him or, if you have fallen away from Him, come back to Him. He is God and will continue to be God because God has no end. As God, He only asks for your faithfulness, truthfulness, and your love. He is longing to have you join His family. Will you?

All that is needed is to ask Jesus Christ, God's Son, to be your Savior. It is a free gift. Nothing you have to do or accomplish, other than to believe and ask Jesus to be Your Savior. He is available at this very moment. You can ask Him right now. He will not say no. He will invite you immediately to be His and a part of God's family from this moment on.

Jesus is calling. He is calling you to come and receive Him as your Savior. This will be the most wonderful decision of your life.

You will never regret it. Come, ask Him now!

ACKNOWLEDGEMENTS

AS I REFLECT ON crafting this book, I think of those who sojourned with me through the process. Those who encouraged me and continued to inspire me to keep going with the project. It only took three years of encouragement but the book is complete. To Eyerus, who never let me waver from God's calling to write this book. She provided me a true story which became one of the chapters. Thank you to my great friend John who read my chapters and provided great insight and critical reshaping when needed. To Mary Jo, who encouraged me to write with only one thought in mind for each sentence. I took inspiration from Hemingway after that and hope his style is reflected in my writing. To my children Keri and Derek who provided great hope and love to me. Never wavering in their commitment to an imperfect dad, who loves them from the depths of my soul.

I dedicate this book to all those who provided me stories by sharing their lives, even though each story was changed. My gratitude to all of you who informed me of what you would do if you were God in a particular situation.

Finally, totally and completely, I dedicate this book to the Lord, who has been my greatest inspiration in authoring this book. The Lord would not allow me rest until it was completed. There was the Holy Spirit who clothed me and immersed himself in me to continue to keep going and finish the book. He would spring up in me to make sure that other matters, life issues, business and projects were a thorn of interference and difficulty until I dedicated myself to finishing this manuscript.

ABOUT THE AUTHOR

JERRY TROYER HAS DEDICATED the last twenty plus years of his life to gaining knowledge, understanding, and education in Christian living and values. He has applied that information in serving the Lord following attending seminary and earning a degree in Christian Counseling. He currently counsels Christians, believers, and seekers. He is an ordained Chaplain, minister and ordained elder. He serves in capacities of working with Marine recruits, mentoring Christians, service at church, and aiding the needy. Jerry is the founder, of Providence a financial literacy service provider. He thrives in the arena of Biblical financial literacy, personal finance, and planned spending. His corporate career included being a lender banker, licensed financial advisor, and small business owner. He has served on many non-profit or charity boards, including being a current co-director of Vessels of Hope Missions.

He graduated from Newburgh Theological Seminary with a Doctor of Divinity degree and a BA in Christian Counseling. He holds a Graduate Degree from Midwest School of Banking, with a major in Banking Administration. He is a graduate of Hamilton University, holding a BA in Business Management, and holds an AA degree in Business Management from Glen Oaks Community College.

He is an ordained Chaplain with Living Shield Ministries.